The Prayer Tradition of Black People

Sister Bell

Prayer Power!

Sept. 6, 1985

God Be with You!

Harold A. Carter

The Prayer Tradition of Black People

Harold A. Carter

GATEWAY PRESS, INC.
Baltimore   1985

THE PRAYER TRADITION OF BLACK PEOPLE

Copyright © 1976
Judson Press, Valley Forge, PA 19481
Second Printing, 1977
Third Printing, Gateway Press, Baltimore, 1982
Fourth Printing, 1984
Fifth Printing, 1985

Bible quotations in this book are taken from *The Holy Bible,* King James Version.

Library of Congress Cataloging in Publication Data

Carter, Harold A.
  The prayer tradition of Black people.

  Bibliography: p. 133.
  Includes index.
  1. Negroes—Religion. 2. Prayer—History.
I. Title.
BR563.N4C37   264'.1   75-35881
ISBN 0-8170-0698-2

Printed in the U.S.A.

Copies of this book may be ordered from:
Harold A. Carter
3501 Sequoia Ave.
Baltimore, MD 21215

To Momma and Daddy
whose Afro-American marriage
of song and prayer
have left in the writer
rivers of amazing
spirit-filled waters.

Foreword

The Prayer Tradition of Black People is, officially, a product of the Martin Luther King Program of Black Church Studies at Colgate Rochester Divinity School, Bexley Hall, and Crozer Theological Seminary. However, in a much larger and more representative sense, it is the product of a whole race and culture, and centuries of oppression and suffering, of faith and victory. That it has been so long in bursting into print has to do with the status of print in Black culture and the status of Black culture, until recently, in colleges and seminaries. We have Harold A. Carter to thank for using the program to facilitate the capture of the tradition, insofar as books can accomplish so great a task. And he may be thanked also for being the living bridge between the oral and written cultures—the authentic product, himself, of the tradition he records, while having acquired the additional identity of the writer/reflector/scholar. In this role as an authentic and achieving Black-culture pastor, as well as reflector and writer about it, Carter is the epitome of what the MLK Program is all about.

This book, therefore, is perhaps the firstfruits to reach print, of a series of eighteen contributions from the King Program, whose purpose it has richly achieved. The history and function of prayer in Black Christianity are well documented but accurately and warmly expressed. The future of an otherwise diminishing art and resource is the more secure because a product of that artful heritage of soul has dared the discipline and borne the burden of translation into a medium at once more stable in a technologically swift-moving world, and a bit alien to it. No Black church leader, lay or clergy, can well afford not to read and be confronted and enriched by *The Prayer Tradition*.

But authentic Christianity grows out of vital life experience, which, no matter how culturally conditioned, has universal human appeal. Our Lord lived in the cultural particularity of oppressed Jews, but his gospel and saving acts are for the whole world. A post-enlightenment Euro-American culture is desperately in need of a white parallel to Black prayer, in which the social a priori acknowledge both the human need to talk with God, literally, and the inability to explain how that communication works in material terms. The mainstream of American religious and social mentality needs also a means of transcending traditionally vested interests and taking care of the kingdom business of liberating persons and peoples. For the purposes of America's cultural majority, there is probably no more stimulating a challenge to and resource for hard-nosed, practical piety than the Black prayer tradition.

A concluding confession may suggest just how much we need the stretch forward and backward which this work represents. I urged appointment of Harold Carter as a King Fellow because of his widely heard broadcasts and the great respect in which they are held. When he declined the suggested topic and chose to write on prayer, I suspected that we had lost access to his greatest possible gift to Black Church Studies. Nothing could have been further from the truth. Even his broadcasts are greatly enriched by his capacity to capture the cry of crushed humanity in the poetry of their prayer heritage, while addressing the most pressing of contemporary issues. Should I ever be called back to service as a local pastor, the "deacons' prayer meeting" before public worship and the midweek service, neither of which I ever did surrender, would be greatly enriched with a sense of purpose and a relationship to roots. And I suspect the same would be the case with a reader/pastor of any denomination or race.

Henry H. Mitchell

Acknowledgments

Every book is a collective endeavor. I owe profound thanks to many. Dr. Robert Keighton, homiletical professor at Crozer Theological Seminary, Chester, Pennsylvania, 1958, first encouraged me in this work. Years later, Dr. C. S. Mann, of St. Mary's Seminary and University, Baltimore, Maryland, provided many rich moments of dialogue and mental stimulation. The shared experience as a Martin Luther King Fellow, studying under the guidance of Dr. Henry Mitchell, who conceived and directed this program in Black Religious Studies at Colgate Rochester Divinity School/Bexley Hall/Crozer Theological Seminary, provided the necessary environment and motivation to complete this work.

Dr. Richard I. McKinney, of Morgan University, Baltimore, Maryland, offered crucial insights and instructive points into formal thesis writing.

New Shiloh Baptist Church was totally supportive of my

endeavors. Mrs. Salome Ratliff, administrative secretary of the church, gave strategic service at the typewriter.

My deepest gratitude goes to my wife, Weptanomah, whose support of my endeavor deepened as the hours of research and writing unfolded. She, more than anyone else, knows the germinal force this initial work has had in my life, and the ongoing desire to continue this demanding task.

Finally, I am grateful to Almighty God who brings every good work to fruition.

Harold A. Carter

Preface

The seed of this undertaking was planted in the bosom of the writer from the religious fires of Black people in the heart of the Black belt of Alabama, in Dallas County. The county seat was located in the city of Selma. Here the writer was born into a family of active church workers, Nathan Mitchell Carter, Sr., and Lillie Belle Carter. Nathan Carter, a minister and theologian, provided a rich fund of Black prayer insights as he pastored Black people in the rural districts of Alabama. Nathan Carter often told his family that prayer was the foundation of his life and the key to all of his accomplishments. His epic prayer experience was how God had heard his petitions at a time when he was in great need. He was married, had four children, was living in a poorly constructed home, and was making less than fifty dollars per month as a teacher and also as a pastor. He was deeply in financial debt, unable to support fully his family, in need of money, and in failing health. On Christmas Day in the year 1942, Nathan

Carter went out on the range line road, leading out from Selma, and prayed to God in front of Little Rock Baptist Church. He petitioned God for four things: (1) that God would provide him with additional funds to pay his debts; (2) that God would provide better housing for his family; (3) that God would promote him from his pastorate at Center Felix Baptist Church, nineteen miles north of Selma, where he had been for thirteen years and felt he could make no more progress; and (4) that God would restore his health and strength. The day after Christmas, Nathan Carter met A. M. Moseley, a ministerial friend, who told him the president of Selma University wished to see him. Moseley related that the Southern Baptist Convention Home Mission Board was prepared to underwrite the salary of two teachers in Christian Religion at Selma University. Nathan Carter was accepted for this work and thus received the answer to his first petition. Within the same week another friend of Selma University, Mrs. Pollard, informed Nathan Carter that she had a home two blocks away from the university and would make it available to him. The transaction was made and the second petition was answered. During the same week an invitation was established for Nathan Carter to preach at the Old Town Baptist Church, where his next pastorate began. The answer to his fourth petition was inherent in solving the other problems. His health was restored. Ever since that Christmas Day, Nathan Carter has made a Pilgrimage in Prayer to that same spot where God heard him in such a mighty way. The influence of this prayer experience, movingly told by the writer's father, has had positive value leading to an intense interest in the prayers of Black people generally.

The writer at an early age became fascinated with the prayers falling from the lips of deacons whose words could literally set the church on holy fire. Here the "mourners'" bench, the front row of the church, became alive with seekers in annual revival services, where mighty prayers of the saints were offered for their salvation. This church experience was also colored by the influence of Lillie Belle Carter, who was gifted with a powerful voice to sing God's praise. Lillie Belle would often sing without piano or organ accompaniment, supported entirely by the tapping of feet on the floor, the nodding and swaying of heads, a shout here and an "amen" there, and the spiritual strength of her voice. This powerful mixture of song and prayer left deep and lasting impressions upon the writer that seek wider expression in this book.

The same influence of Black prayers heard in the rural and city churches of Dallas County was also felt by the writer on weekdays at Selma University, Selma, Alabama. This Black religious school was founded by ministers one hundred years ago and was the school where the writer spent the first ten years of his academic life. Daily chapel services, at 9:00 A.M., were an absolute requirement in this school. Here the writer had the experience of hearing prayers of ministers and laymen daily and also had the opportunity to hear countless prayers of Black people who came to this school from neighboring states. In those early days, the writer noticed a certain consistency in the prayers of Black people. The common thread of language and imagery of Black prayers, heard day after day, by young and older students, said something about a powerful folk tradition. Now, years later, the writer approaches this task of lifting up the prayer tradition of Black people, knowing it has served as a spiritual platform on which this people have gathered from all ranks of our society to seek their own full liberation and to work toward building the beloved community of all people.

This work, therefore, represents a lifelong ambition. It is the hope of this writer that the Black prayer tradition can be identified and lifted up for the serious, ongoing concern of Black people particularly and all men generally. There is also the desire that this work lift up the Black prayer tradition, so that it will command the scholarly attention of theologians and the serious concern of all persons who seek a fuller understanding of the Black religious experience in the New World.

Contents

1

Introduction

The prayer tradition of Black people is a great reservoir of faith and culture and has had incalculable influence in shaping the lives of every new generation. It is a tradition nurtured in the praise houses and fields of the South and passed on in the oral prayers and narratives of slaves and their descendants. It is seen in the total folk heritage of Black people, surviving to this day. It is part of a life-style of a people quick to say, "Amen and praise God" and the oft-repeated phrase "If the Lord wills it."

This study is pursued in the hope of lifting up the Black prayer tradition as a spiritual force necessary for the Black community's continued growth and a vital contribution to the community of mankind. The use of the term "Black people" in this study will refer to a people of African ancestry, originally slaves in the New World, having a color as a mark, sharing a common bondage and heritage, and living under segregation and oppression. Primary focus will be given to the recorded and oral utterances of this people in public prayer, from the days of slavery to the present time. Interviews with elderly Black persons and other field research will augment this effort.

The act of prayer in the Black tradition reflects a personal involvement that colors one's total response to and expectations from life. This heritage of prayer is identifiable among Black people in language, style, imagery, and spirit. Its oral tradition touches upon the Black community at large but is particularly seen in the Black, Protestant, free churches, where spontaneous congregational participation is a normal part of worship. Therefore, Black persons who share in denominational bodies made up primarily of a White constituency are not the focal point of this study. The writer is also aware that a minority group of Blacks has argued that prayer is a form of human resignation to one's conditions, deliberately propagated by the White man's version of the Christian religion to enslave the Black man. They have openly rebelled against the practice of prayer. However, the impact of the Black prayer tradition has been so powerful that is has colored the life-style of this people and has surfaced as a spiritual pillar in support of all their efforts in liberation and community development.

This work will draw upon a variety of scholarly sources and on the personal experience and knowledge of the writer. Some of the insights were gained from two trips to West Africa. Lectures, tapes, and field studies by African scholars will support observations made while there. A great deal of attention will also be given to the published narratives of ex-slaves. Among the studies of slave songs and religious thought to be considered are works by Benjamin Mays, Howard Thurman, Miles Mark Fisher, and John Lovell. African sociological studies by Phoebe Ottenberg have been consulted, and serious attention has been given to the theological studies of African culture by John Mbiti. Histories of America's Black past by Carter Woodson and autobiographies by influential Black persons will strengthen the thesis of this book. Every effort will be made to see this prayer tradition as it surfaces in and outside the organized church, so as to show its influence in shaping the lives of Black people. Extensive thought will be given to the Black prayer experience as an undergirder of the liberation efforts of Black people and the civil rights movement under the leadership of the late Martin Luther King, Jr.

How is it the prayers of Black people today are so similar to the prayers uttered during the days of slavery? Is there some reason why this prayer language is almost universally accepted by Black people? One answer is that a common ground of suffering, imposed by the bondage of slavery, created a mold that made for a common sharing of experience in prayer. From this common heritage, prayer has served as a source of inner release and personal fulfillment. This tradition can certainly go on to serve as a model for the Black person seeking a full and complete participation in the family of humanity.

This research is entered with long-standing enthusiasm. The writer has known the Black person's verbal response to God in word, song, and chant from boyhood days in Alabama. Through this act Black people sought to find meaning for life by communicating with God. The spontaneity, vivid imagery, beautiful metaphors, and synonyms that emerged in these prayers were truly moving. No one could ignore the mysterious attitude of reverence that accompanied the prayer event. The brother, the sister, was literally talking to God. He or she may have been bowed down on their knees or may have been standing, rubbing hands together with head pointed like a sculptured rock toward heaven. In the minds of Black people in the church, Jesus was now on the main line, and you could tell him what you want. This Black prayer tradition produced popular saints who could "really talk to de Lawd." Here prayer was more than a word spoken; it was an event to be experienced. The spirit of what happened was as important as the words spoken. This prayer tradition, akin to the Black song tradition, provided opportunity for everyone to participate at a level of private and corporate significance in the ongoing life of the Black religious community.

The Black prayer tradition must be seriously rethought and consciously revived if this valuable source of traditional spiritual power is to serve the ongoing needs of the Black person in today's world. The children of Black people need to know this past, filled with prayers that related so meaningfully to life. Black ministers need to know this history, so that they might use this creative prayer tradition in forging a more beloved community among Black sons and daughters today and tomorrow. Indeed, it is the writer's hope that all persons who read this book will find a new appreciation for the distinctive prayers of Black people and discover how these prayers have made a lasting contribution in the total development of Black people in the New World.

2

African Heritage in the Black Prayer Tradition

The African religious tradition has left many traces of its native influence upon the life-style of Black people in America. One of these basic influences has been the habit and impact of prayer. The common practice of prayers among Black slaves in the New World is distinctly noticed in the early days of the Black people's recorded life as slaves. Their understanding of God was informed by an African theology that naturally accepted the Being and supremacy of God as a fact obviously known and never debated. There was no distinction made between the sacred and the secular in their native African background. The presence of God was experienced as an intimate part of all life. This basic African religious background revealed itself in the religious practices of slaves as they sought both openly and secretly to find meaning and personhood in life.

God, Ritual and Practice

In West African religions, one will find the idea of God expressed in proverbs, epigrams, songs, prayers, names, myths, stories, and religious ceremonies. One will not find long drawn-out dissertations about God. One will find an oral tradition, and it is expected that each person will have a normal relationship with God. There is an Ashanti proverb which states, "No one shows a child the Supreme Being." [1] Everyone is expected to know God's existence by normal natural instinct. It is this instinct that relates directly to prayer.

The people of Africa have traditionally lived close to the land. Prayers to God relate directly to the need for rain, fertility, and welfare of humans, cattle, and fields. Since animals and plants constitute food for humans, it is not surprising that Africans have many religious ceremonies associated with them.

In the act of worship, the African approaches God. This act is aided by sacrifices, offerings, prayers, and invocations. God is the one who makes the sun rise and set, the rain fall, the mountains quake, and the rivers overflow. He heals the sick, helps the barren, and aids those in distress.

The African prays at the beginning of his principal occupations, such as sowing the fields and going out to fish. God permeates the totality of life for the African and acts through all his creation.

While studying in Africa in the summer of 1972, the writer observed fishermen in coastal villages in Ghana in prayer and offering libations before going out to sea. The Ibo people of Nigeria were observed offering prayers at the beginning and the end of each day. Government officials, scholars, and ordinary citizens were comfortable and active in prayer. Many jitney buses had prayers painted on the front and on the rear. Prayer was literally everywhere.

The African associates the Supreme God with the sky or heaven. While there are able gods and spirits who make contact with humans and serve as intermediaries, the Supreme God dwells on high.

As far as written sources available are concerned, all African peoples associate God with the sky or heaven, in one way or another. There are those who say He reigns there; the majority think that He lives there; and

[1] John S. Mbiti, *African Religions and Philosophy,* John S. White, ed. (New York: Frederick A. Praeger Publishers, 1969), p. 29.

some even identify Him with the sky, or consider it to be His chief manifestation.[2]

One will observe a system of community in Africa where priests, priestesses, elders, and priest-doctors are venerated as being able to make contact with the power of God. Libations to God are offered by the elders, the priests, or the local king. One does not or should not approach God alone but does so through special persons.

> Priests are reported in many societies. As a rule, they are formally trained and commissioned (ordained), they may be male or female, hereditary or otherwise. Their duties include making sacrifices, offerings and prayers, conducting both public and private rites and ceremonies, giving advice, performing judicial or political functions, caring for temples and shrines where these exist, and above all fulfilling their office as religious intermediaries between man and God.[3]

The Mende people of Sierra Leone, West Africa, are known to pray directly to God, making use of intermediary spirits and the living/dead, ending their prayers with the words: "God willing! God willing!"[4] A study of their way of life reveals a high sense of prayer consciousness. They believe the living dead can influence the good will of God. One of their prayers reads thusly:

> O God, let it reach to (through?) Kenei Momo,
> Let it reach to (through?) Nduawo,
> Let it reach all our forefathers who are in Thy hands.[5]

Mary Cable tells the story of some Mende people who mutinied and captured their own slave ship, called the *Amistad,* and eventually landed in Connecticut.[6] This group of Africans, seeking their freedom, gained widespread notoriety for their legal fight to remain as free combatants and not be pressed into slavery. Many professors and students at Yale Divinity School thought them to be heathens, unable to approach God, but such was not the case. Mary Cable writes:

[2]*Ibid.,* p. 52.
[3]*Ibid.,* p. 68.
[4]*Ibid.,* p. 63.
[5]*Ibid.*
[6]The *Amistad* case is historically important, since the committee formed to aid these Africans eventually developed into the American Missionary Association that did mission work in many parts of the world and led in establishing many Black colleges, such as Hampton Institute, Talladega College, Fisk University, and Howard University, to name a few still active and flourishing.

The Mende of Cinque's day believed in a Supreme Being, creator of all, who punished or rewarded. Thus they had no difficulty in accepting the God [the New God Jesus Christ] offered them in New Haven. The Mende God was a more remote and unapproachable figure than the God of the Christians. However, he could be approached "through channels," as it were: one's immediate ancestors could be asked to convey a petition to a more remote ancestor, who told it to the spirits of the hills and water, who told it to God. . . .[7]

The influence of this African tradition was seen in the recent retirement of Elder H. Thomas, a native of the West Indies, who founded the Pentecostal Church on the island of Bermuda. Elder Thomas was asked how he came to found this, the oldest Black church on the island. He responded:

I came with my parents to Bermuda from the West Indies. My parents in the West Indies had been brought there directly from West Africa. They came to Bermuda seventy-four years ago looking for better living conditions. Here we had prayer meetings every night. One night, the eldest person in our prayer group got filled with the spirit, and came to me, and all the elders came and laid their hands on my head and told me through prayer that I was the one to found a church.[8]

This interesting piece of history throws light on the kind of native African influence that survived the big sea and was ready to be nurtured in new places and on new soil. We look now at some of these influences during the days of slavery.

Early Traces of African Influence During Slavery

The slaves' lives in the New World were rigidly predetermined from sunup to sundown. However, from "sundown to sunup" they did have some moments for creating and recreating themselves in the light of their existence.

In North America before the second quarter of the eighteenth century, little pressure was put upon the slaves to become Christians. As long as the slaves worked well and were not unruly they were left alone. After that, for the remainder of the century, the efforts that were made to convert the slaves were sporadic, and while they resulted in getting most slaves to adopt the outward forms of Christianity, the relative neglect also allowed

---

[7]Mary Cable, *Black Odyssey* (New York: The Viking Press, 1971), pp. 110-111.
[8]Statement by Elder Thomas, personal interview with writer, December 5, 1973.

the slaves to develop Christianity's interior meanings and practices in their own way.[9]

Clearly, only halfhearted effort was made by slave masters to superimpose formal religion on the slave. The narratives of ex-slaves reveal a kind of individual initiative in finding God, relating to him in prayer. While they often gathered as a group, from plantation to plantation, cabin to cabin, each person was free to experience God in his or her own particular way. A few expressions follow:

> Sometimes us slip off an' have a little prayer meetin' by usse'ves in a ole house wid a dirt flo. Dey'd git happy an' shout an' couldn't nobody hyar 'em, 'caze dey didn't make no fuss on de dirt flo', an' one stan' in de do' an' watch. Some folks put de head in de wash pot to pray, an' pray easy, an' somebody be watchin' for de overseer. Us git whupped for ev'ything iffen hit was public knowed.[10]

> Dey was rough people and dey treat ev'rybody rough. . . . No suh, we never goes to church. Times we sneaks in de woods and prays de Lawd to make us free and times one of de slaves got happy and made a noise dat dey heerd at de big house and den de overseer come and whip us 'cause we prayed de Lawd to set us free.[11]

> Massa never 'lowed us slaves go to church but they have big holes in the field they gits down in and prays. They done that way 'cause the white folks didn't want them to pray. They used to pray for freedom.[12]

It is clear that the slaves had to practice their religion and offer their prayers secretly. Some scattered slave masters did permit some degree of religious participation, but they were exceptions and not the general rule. Refusals to stop praying revealed the strong tendency of the slaves' Afro-religious inheritance to find some supreme object of praise in whom to celebrate the gift of life.

The Praise House

The praise house was a building used widely in the days of slavery, where slaves would gather nightly for the purpose of song, dance, and prayer. Many religious conversion experiences of slaves occurred in these buildings. The praise house as a special place of celebration definitely had a West African background. In village after village in

[9] George P. Rawick, *The American Slave: A Composite Autobiography*, vol. 1, *From Sundown to Sunup* (Westport, Conn.: Greenwood Publishing Company, 1972), pp. 32-33.
[10] Rawick, *op. cit.*, vol. 6, *Alabama and Indiana Narratives*, p. 433.
[11] Quoted in Rawick, *op. cit.*, vol. 1, p. 35.
[12] Quoted in *ibid.*

West Africa, the writer found many houses erected for the specific purpose of song, dance, libations, and praise to God. Miles Mark Fisher sees a direct link between the praise houses of West Africa and the development of the Black church in America.[13]

There was a freedom in these praise houses for singing, praying, shouting, and the experience of conversion.

> The "praise house," developed on the Sea Islands, it seems, was a chapel attended only by slaves. "About fifteen feet square, begrimed with smoke and dirt," there were few windows in it, and the pastor was likely to be a slave. At Pine Grove, on St. Helena's Island, the "praise house" was merely a "rather larger and nicer hut than the others." In the house the slaves, mainly field hands, prayed and sang, became "convicted" of sin, or even "got religion," without the restrictive presence of white persons.[14]

The formative impact of prayer in the "praise house" was strong and abiding.

> Very likely more than half the population of a plantation is gathered together. Let it be evening, and a light woodfire burns red before the door of the house and on the hearth. For some time one can hear, though at a good distance, the vociferous exhortation of a prayer of the presiding elder or of the brother who has a gift that way. . . .[15]

The slave time "ring dance" was also an integral part of this praise-house celebration. Bishop D. A. Payne, of the African Methodist Church, an eyewitness to this dance, was told that the slaves believed no one could be converted without the ring and the dance.

> Said I, "You might sing till you fell down dead and you would fail to convert a single sinner." He [the leader of the band] replied: "The Spirit of God works upon people in different ways. At camp meetings there must be a ring here, a ring there, a ring over yonder, or sinners will not be converted."[16]

The ring dance was a shuffle to the tune of some spiritual. Many times a special group of singers or shouters would keep the rhythm and sounds flowing. "Song and dance are alike extremely energetic

[13]Miles Mark Fisher, *Negro Slave Songs in the United States* (New York: Cornell University Press, 1953), p. 186.

[14]Bertram Wilbur Doyle, *The Etiquette of Race Relations in the South* (Port Washington, N.Y.: Kennikat Press, Inc., 1968), p. 49.

[15]Joseph R. Washington, Jr., *Black Sects and Cults* (New York: Doubleday & Company, Inc., 1972), pp. 74-75.

[16]Charles Spencer Smith, *A History of the African Methodist Episcopal Church* (Philadelphia: Book Concern of the A.M.E. Church, 1922), p. 126.

and often, when the shout lasts into the middle of the night, the monotonous thud, thud, of the feet prevents sleep within half a mile of the praise house." [17] The praise house with its dance, its song, and prayer clearly did not come from White influence. There was a freedom of religious practice in the praise house that reflected African origins seeking some creative expression in the New World.

In the praise house were certain characteristics that would endure in the Black prayer tradition. The leadership of one who apparently has the gift for prayer certainly emerges. The close association between prayer and song is evident. The way of making prayer an event, involving one's entire body, is seen in these nightly meetings. The nightly moments for relatively free worship helped to form the soulful environment out of which the Black prayer life grew.

The Pot

The pot, like the praise house, was closely associated with the religious practices of Black slaves in the New World. The pot was used as a way of catching the sound of the slave's songs and prayers, so as to prevent the master from hearing the person at worship and learning the true importance of the utterances to God. The reason for the use of the pot in this fashion during the days of slavery may be found in the slave's West African heritage.

> In West Africa, pots were a regular part of the ceremonial paraphernalia. Herskovits tells us that in Dahomian funerals where all the ancestors, including those who died in America, are remembered, there is a little pot for each ancestor into which a young chick is placed as a sacrifice. The *loa* in Haitian vodun are also "kept" in pots.
> The pot is a ubiquitous item associated in West Africa with the gods, very often with those important river spirits who are seen as being the closest to men. [18]

The writer witnessed the use of pots around a shrine in Abanze, Ghana. These pots, containing sea water, were used in libations to various deities, bearing on the fisherman's life.

Obviously a shift of meaning occurred in the use of pots in the days of slavery. During slavery, it was believed that the pot, turned upside down, would somehow catch the sound of the prayers and shouts and

[17] Washington, *op. cit.,* p. 75.
[18] Rawick, *op. cit.,* vol. 1, p. 42.

would not disturb the master or reveal unapproved worship. One ex-slave reveals this fact in his narrative:

> They used to have prayer meetings. In some places that they have prayer meetings they would turn pots down in the middle of the floor to keep the white folks from hearing them sing and pray and testify, you know. Well, I don't know where they learned to do that. I kinda think the Lord put them things in their mind to do for themselves, just like he helps us Christians in other ways. Don't you think so?[19]

Another ex-slave gives a more descriptive account:

> . . . they would get a big ole wash kettle and put it right outside the door, and turn it bottom upwards to get the sound, then they would go in the house and sing and pray, and the kettle would catch the sound. I spose they would kinda have it propped up so the sound would get under it.[20]

Older persons in the writer's hometown, Selma, Alabama, would often collect rainwater in pots. An explanation was generally given that rainwater was pure, was from God, and had healing powers.

It is clear that the memory of the pot did not die among southern Blacks. Jesse Owens, the Black Olympic runner, talking about his father's illiteracy, wrote: "Yet if Henry Owens never was able to read the words of his religion, at least he didn't have to dig a hole in the ground or put a kitchen pot over his head to pray."[21]

Field Prayers

In that long period before Christianity was deliberately preached to the slaves by missionaries, the slaves wove into their lives a close companionship with God on their own cultural terms. Prayers were born in the field, where the slaves spent so much of their lives. They were primarily prayers for freedom and for one's children to see a better day. The duties of the slaves in the field provided objects to enrich the imagery of their prayers.

As a plowman holding the reins of the beast, he asked God to "try the reins of my mind and lead me in a straight path." The need for holding the plow and going forward caused him to pray, "Lord, help me to keep my eyes on Jesus and never turn back." The long row of the field became the "row of life" that would one day be over. Planting

[19] *Ibid.*, vol. 18, *Unwritten History of Slavery*, p. 24.
[20] *Ibid.*, p. 35.
[21] Rawick, *op. cit.*, vol. 1, p. 43.

and reaping were a positive object lesson on praying today and expecting a blessing from God tomorrow.

This was not a period of long, flowery prayers. The slaves' utterances to God usually flowed as a natural response to life's basic needs. In a deep sense, life in its totality was an experience of their wonder before God and of God's care for them in a hard land.

> God started on me when I was a little boy. I used to grieve a lot over my mother. She had been sold away from me and taken a long way off. One evening I was going through the woods to get the cows. I was walking along thinking about Mama and crying. Then a voice spoke to me and said, "Blessed art thou. An obedient child shall live out the fullness of his days." I got scared because I did not know who it was that spoke nor what he meant. But from this time on I thought more about God and my soul and started to praying as best I knew how. It went on this way until I was about grown. I would pray awhile and then stop and forget God.[22]

This was a typical slave experience. A mother was sold away, leaving a child to grieve. The intensity of the grief created a personality receptive to the one big force available to the slave, Spiritual Power! There were no theological dogmas to block intimate reception. No latent church traditions stood in the way. The slave was free, even in physical bondage, to ponder his existence before God.

The outdoors that served for prayers of petition would eventually serve for prayerful rejoicing.

> "Freedom—Aunt Mariah Jackson was freed at Dublin, Mississippi. She said she was out in the field working. A great big white man come, jumped upon a log and shouted, 'Freedom! Freedom!' They let the log they was toting down; six, three on a side, had holt of a hand stick toting a long heavy log. They was clearing up new ground. He told them they was free. They went to the house. They cooked and et and thanked God. Some got down and prayed, some sung. They had a time that day. They got the banjo and fiddle and set out playing. Some got in the big road just walking. She said they had a time that day."[23]

The Special Tree and Praying Ground

The intimacy the Black people found in prayer is reflected historically in their having some special place for prayer. For many, this place was a tree where God's presence was felt in some deeper and

[22]Clifton H. Johnson, ed., *God Struck Me Dead* (Philadelphia: Pilgrim Press, 1969), p. 19. Reprinted with permission. Copyright © 1969 United Church Press.
[23]Rawick, *op. cit.,* vol. 10, *Arkansas Narratives,* part 6, pp. 143-144.

more intimate way. The writer discovered while in West Africa that many Ashanti people believe certain spirits inhabit certain trees and that these trees provide a sacred place for one to communicate with God. "The Ashanti have spirits that animate trees, rivers, animals, charms and the like; and below these are family spirits thought to be ever present, and to act as guardians." [24] It is not surprising to find so many slaves having a special place, even a special tree or spot by some river or stream, where meaning was found by meeting God. Indeed, one of the favorite lines in the traditional Black prayer language says to God, "Thank you, Lord, for leaving me in a Bible-reading country, where I can pick and choose my own praying ground."

The slave whose narrative follows certainly had a praying ground.

> That night I went to my regular praying place. I usually prayed behind a big beech tree a little distance from the house, and often during the night, when I would feel to pray, I would get out of bed and go to this tree. That night I said, "Lord, if I am praying right, let me hear a dove mourn three times." While I was praying I went off in a trance, and I saw myself going up a broad, hilly road through the woods. When I was nearly to the top I saw a big dog. I got scared and started to run back, but something urged me on. The dog was chained to a big block, I found out when I got closer, and though she tried to get to me, I passed out of her reach. I came then to a tree like a willow, and there I heard a dove mourn three times. [25]

This prayer experience made a specific request of God: "Lord, if I am praying right, let me hear a dove mourn three times." There developed in Black prayers a strong tendency to speak and think directly with God. The big dog no doubt directly personified evil in this trance. The dog was held in low esteem in traditional African societies. The dove, however, was seen as an angel of God, a messenger of goodwill. So the answer and deliverance were equally direct.

Just recently, an elderly woman was heard singing in a revival meeting in Charlotte, North Carolina:

> I'm gonna weep by a willow
> and mourn like a dove
> I'm getting ready to leave this world.

The elderly woman obviously had her prayer ground located by a

24 Mbiti, op. cit., p. 87.
25 Johnson, op. cit., pp. 20-21.

willow tree. She sensed her days on earth were few. The experience of prayer she had by the willow was celebrated in song in the act of worship.

In an interview with a cross section of deacons of New Shiloh Baptist Church, Baltimore, Maryland, a specific question was asked: "Do any of you men remember your parents or grandparents having any specific place for prayer? Several answers follow:

> Yes. I'm from Virginia. Every afternoon my mother would go to a certain spot in the woods, and occasionally us boys would follow her; she didn't know it.
> I was back home last year and I went looking for that spot. I wanted to pray in the same place.
>
> My grandmother used to go down to the spring twice a day, morning and evening. Whenever she would go and stay too long, my mother would say, "Sidney, go yonder and get your grandmother with the water; I know she is down there praying."

The intimate relationship between prayer and field is suggestive of how the slave saw God working through nature to provide sustaining power for people. One ex-slave reported the following prayer experience, in which her mother prayed for a place for her children to pray in.

> But I do remember how she used to take us children and kneel down in front of the fireplace and pray. She'd pray that the time would come when everybody could worship the Lord under their own vine and fig tree ... all of them free. It's come to me lots of times since. There she was a' praying, and on other plantations women was a' praying. All over the country the same prayer was being prayed. Guess the Lord done heard the prayer and answered it.[26]

In the New World, Black people found a cathedral in the field and in the woods to make their petitions to God. They had the philosophy expressed by Charlie Smith, the oldest ex-slave known in the New World, who recently celebrated his 132nd birthday. Charlie Smith was asked, "What is your formula for a long life and good health?" Charlie responded, "I've joined everything a person can join but the church. You can live right without joining a church. The Lord will hear your prayers just as good anywhere as he will in the church."[27]

[26] Rawick, *op. cit.,* vol. 10, part 6, p. 64.
[27] *The Afro-American* (Baltimore), August 24, 1974, p. 18.

Prayer for the slaves was the important spiritual pursuit of their lives. In the praise house they danced, shouted, and prayed at night. In the day, behind a hoe, pushing a saw in the forest or clearing a field, the need of God was truly uppermost in their minds. They saw their God revealing to them things in dreams, visions, songs, and prayers. While no massive missionary movement had been directed toward reaching the slaves, a movement of even greater proportion was taking place in their souls. They gradually became acquainted with the Bible, receiving theological and biblical influences that had far-reaching impact upon their lives. This impact was seen in their concept of God and of themselves. The name of Jesus, the power of the church, and the hope of eternal life were now pillars of salvation. Prayer and praise in a far greater sense provided for them a vital source for the affirmation of life.

3

Theological Influences Within the Black Prayer Tradition

During the days of slavery, many Blacks found opportunity to learn something about God's Word and the nature of the church through contact with their masters. House servants were occasionally trained in basic educational skills. Carriage drivers heard sermons from the balconies of plantation churches. Some owners insisted on their slaves having some form of church and even read the Bible to them.

> Evah Sunda mawnin Marster Louis would have all us slaves tuh de house while he would sing an pray an read de Bible tuh us all.[1]

Many masters sought the church as a defense to hold the slave in place. So much of preaching to the slave consisted of negatives, such

---

[1] George P. Rawick, ed., *The American Slave: A Composite Autobiography,* vol. 10, *Arkansas Narratives,* part 5 (Westport: Greenwood Publishing Company, 1972), p. 149.

as, "Don't steal your master's chickens; don't kill his hogs; and obey him in all things." The amazing fact is that the slave saw through this sham religion and identified with the relevant forces found in Scripture.

Theological Influences from the Old Testament

The Old Testament, with its redemptive history of a people once in slavery, was sufficient proof to the slaves that they would see a better day. So much of their prayer language was molded from the imagery, the concrete expressions, and the chosen-people relationship Israel had with their God. The basic prayer language shaped in these early days would last through the years as the formative language of the Black prayer tradition.

A gentleman of eighty-six years by the name of Washington Banks recalled that his father was an oysterman and that he was the eldest grandchild and grew up under his grandparents' guidance.

> Every night I doze off, my grandmother would tell me, "Don't you forget what I told you." She would wake me up all through the night telling me, "Don't you forget what I done told you."
>
> It happened in the fall of the year. I was not yet converted, and my grandmother would not let me forget what she told me. The last time she woke me up, I doze back off to sleep and commence to hearing a voice in my ears ringing! "Thank God, you've been redeemed!" That was 4:00 A.M. I told my grandmother who said to me, "Get up from here and go and tell your uncles and relatives, you been redeemed!" Right away my relatives began rejoicing with me, "Thank God, you've been redeemed!"

Brother Banks was asked to recite the old-time prayer which he learned from his grandmother. His reply follows:

> I thank Thee, Lawd, for sparing me to see this morning, the blood running warm in my veins, the activity of my limbs and the use of my tongue. I thank Thee for raiment and for food, and above all, I thank Thee for the gift of Thy darling Son Jesus, who came all the way from heaven down to this low ground of sorrow, who died upon the cross, that "whosoever believeth upon Him should not perish but have everlasting life."
>
> Our Lawd, our Heavenly Master, we ask Thee to teach us. Guide us in the way we know not. Give us more faith and a better understanding and a closer walk to Thy bleeding side.
>
> I have a faith to believe you are the same God that was in the days that are past and gone. Thou heard Elijah prayed in the cleft of the mountain.

Thou heard Paul and Silas in jail. Thou heard the three Hebrew children in the fiery furnace. I have a faith to believe that you have once heard me pray, when I was laying and lugging 'round about the gates of hell, no eye to pity me, no arm to save me. Thou reached down your long arm of protection, snatched my soul from the midst of eternal burning. Thou placed me in de rock and placed a new song in my mouth. Thou told me to go, and you would go with me; open my mouth, and you would speak for me.

For that cause we call upon you at this hour. And while we call upon Thee, we ask you please don't go back in Glory, neither turn a deaf ear to our call. But turn down the kindness of a listening ear, catch our moans and our groans, and take 'dem home to the High Heavens. We plead bold one thing more, if 'tis Thy glorious will, I pray Thee.

Oh, Lord, our Heavenly Master, we ask Thee please to search our hearts. Tie the reins of our minds. If thou see anything laying and lugging around our hearts, not your right hand planted and neither pleasing to Thy sight, we ask Thee to remove it by the brightness of your coming, cast it in the sea of forgiveness, where it will never rise up against us in this world, neither condemn us at the bar of judgment, if it 'tis Thy glorious will, I pray Thee.

Oh, God, our Heavenly Father, we ask Thee to please make us a better servant in the future than we have been in the past, and may our last days be our best days.

We thank Thee, Our Heavenly Father, for what you have done for us in days that past and gone, and what you are doing at this present moment. I know you have been good to me, because you have brought me a mighty long ways. Through many dangers, toils, and snares I have already come. 'Twas grace that brought me safe thus far, and grace will lead me on.

Oh, Lord, our Heavenly Master, will you please have mercy; please remember the sick and the afflicted, the poor and those in hospitals, bodies racked in pain, scorched with parching fever; have mercy on them if 'tis Thy glorious will, I pray Thee.

Oh, Lord, my Heavenly Master, remember this weak and unprofitable servant made the attempt to bow before Thee. Go behind me as a protecting Angel, and by my side as a safeguard. And when we have did all assigned to our hands to do, this old world can afford us a home no longer, may we look back and see a well-spent life and just before a joyful hour, that we may be able to sing praise to the Father, Son, One God, world without end. My soul say Amen, Amen, Amen![2]

This prayer is quoted in full due to its basic language, style, imagery, and biblical influences, so common in Black prayers. The most obvious of these influences are the almighty attributes of God.

[2] Statement by Washington Banks, eighty-six years of age, born in Gloucester County, Virginia; deacon in Gethsemane Baptist Church, Baltimore, Maryland, November 15, 1973.

Almighty God Concept

The nature and being of God in the Black prayer tradition are best understood when one pictures God as a heavenly Father who is all powerful, who rules the universe, and who controls all people. Almost always the traditional Black prayer opens with a line addressed specifically to "Almighty God." God is often pictured as the one who "sits high and looks low and knows every thought and action of man." He is also seen in Black prayers as being "too high to get over, too low to get under, too wide to get around, so that one comes to God through the door." Over and over again, God is seen in this prayer tradition as being able to "open doors no man can close, and close doors no man can open. He can build up where no man can tear down, and can tear down where no man can build up." All of these prayer lines are deeply rooted in the language of traditional Black prayers and may be heard repeatedly.

Benjamin E. Mays summarizes the ideas of God in Black prayer as follows:

> God is in heaven. He is all powerful—the source of all things even to allowing us to go to bed and to rise in the morning. In allowing us to do this, He displays mercy. God is a rock in a weary land and a shelter in a mighty storm. All that happens is God's will. God is a partial God who is to be feared and appeased. He does things arbitrarily, apparently for no other reason than the fact that He is all powerful and can do what He pleases.[3]

Black people believed that a personal relationship with God was absolutely necessary. God had to be known at this level, so that the supportive sense of God's presence could provide a lift for life's burdens and encounters. Therefore, the Black people saw God rocking them to sleep at night and awakening them in time and not into eternity every day. Knowing God and doing God's will also provided some sense of security against the many known and unknown cruel forces of life. This feeling was expressed in the following prayer lines:

> Oh, Father, you are a good God, because some are lying on their beds of affliction, some are behind prison bars, some are in the hospital, and

---

[3] Benjamin E. Mays, *The Negro's God* (New York: Russell & Russell, a Division of Atheneum Publishers, Inc., 1968), p. 83.

some are sleeping in their graves; yet, we have been wonderfully blessed with health.[4]

There runs through these prayers the firm belief that health, life, and security from disease come from God. God can extend life and health to whom he will. Those who are fortunate to receive God's blessings are under obligation to praise and thank him for that which they have received.

The Black person's sense of God is essentially gained through experience. God for her or him is not the God of speculation. He is the God who acts in life. He is the one who "spared me to see this morning, the blood still running warm in my veins." He has taught me, guided me, and even placed his word in my wondering mind. He is the God who "heard Elijah in the cleft of the mountain" and certainly hears me now.

It is God who "makes a better servant out of me in the future than I have been in the past." He fights for me, guides, protects, counsels, and keeps me.

Following are two illustrations of the kind of protection and care God offers his own:

> Oh, Lord, come down here and bless our souls. . . . You know we down here are sometimes down and sometimes up; sometimes standing wringing our hands wondering what we must do. Oh, Lord, have mercy on us, I pray. Lord, you remembered Daniel in the Lion's Den, You saved the three Hebrew children, and I know You have heard me pray day after day and I know You will hear me today if I pray right. . . . Oh Lord, have mercy upon us. You know we need You down here. We need You wherever we go to lead us, down here where men and women are so sinful.[5]

> Oh Lord, we are begging you to come by here, front and fight our battle. We are living in a mean world and can't do nothing without you. Lord, we know if you come and be with us, the devil and all his enemies can do us no harm.[6]

The almighty God was real to Black people. Those who could have a personal relationship with him could assure themselves of a friend who "sticketh closer than a brother." They were now members of the Chosen People of God.

[4] *Ibid.,* p. 84.
[5] *Ibid.*
[6] Statement by Deacon Sidney Johnson in worship, Baltimore, Maryland, January 5, 1974.

Chosen People Concept

The self-affirmation of Black people has drawn great strength from the Chosen-People concept. Just as God chose Israel and brought the Israelites out of Egypt, so God has chosen the Black people and brought them out of bondage. "They have always tried to kill us out. . . . If we had not been a chosen race of the Almighty God, we would have been gone long ago."[7]

The biblical text "Princes shall come out of Egypt; Ethiopia shall soon stretch out her hands unto God" has had more than poetic meaning for Black people. Over and over again, Black people saw their own bondage and their eventual pilgrimage to freedom's land as they saw the struggle of Israel wandering through the desert en route to Canaan. They knew they needed the protecting hand of God to make the journey successfully. So they prayed to God, "Go behind me as a protecting angel, and on before me as a safeguard." This biblical analogy to their own situation was a fact of Scripture, and they used it.

> And the Lord went before them by day in a pillar of a cloud, to lead them along the way; and by night in a pillar of fire, to give them light; to go by day and night (Exodus 13:21).

The slaves found meaningful servanthood in being God's chosen people. This sense of the chosen-race concept gave them a sense of security and daily protection, and it provided a sense of racial pride. A slave could now approach God as a "humble unprofitable servant who has made the attempt to bow before a heavenly Father." Their natural predicament, involving a condition of physical bondage to an earthly master, was uniquely transformed in prayer language to that of unprofitable servants, who bow before a heavenly master.

C. J. Washington, a minister of Richmond, Virginia, uttered this basic thought in prayer when he prayed in an Emancipation Proclamation service:

> And O' God, let us not forget, let us always remember, as the children of Israel, "The Lord hast done great things for us," we, too, can say, "The Lord hast done great things for us whereof we are glad."[8]

---

[7] Mays, op. cit., p. 82.
[8] Statement by C. J. Washington, pastor, in prayer at Trinity Baptist Church, Richmond, Virginia, January 1, 1974.

Ancestral Reinforcement

West African religions strongly believe in and practice the veneration of the living dead. One's ancestors live on in the spiritual world and can be spiritually communicated with for strength and power in life's day-by-day journey.

The Hebrew prays to "the God of Abraham, Isaac, and Jacob." The Black person prays to the God who led "my Mother, my Father all the way." A song strongly conveys this message:

> Let Jesus lead you. Let Jesus lead you.
> Let Jesus lead you, all the way.
> All the way from earth to heaven,
> Let Jesus lead you all the way.
>
> He led my mother, He led my father,
> He led my sister all the way, etc.[9]

The ancestral influence is seen at several levels. Like the Hebrews, the Black people often pray to the God of "Abraham, Isaac, and Jacob." Since they are God's "chosen people" in the New World, they have no problem identifying with the biblical characters Abraham, Isaac, and Jacob. They were the "fathers" of a suffering people and were easily adopted by Black slaves as "fathers" worthy of veneration.

The common melting pot of slavery, suffering, and physical bondage created a life-style in the Black people's minds for them to look back on their "fathers" for strength and resolve. The familiar line in the slave spiritual "Swing Low, Sweet Chariot" says:

> "If you get there before I do,
> Tell all my friends I'm coming, too."

This line suggests a vital relationship between those persons who still are making life's pilgrimage and those who have departed these shores. C. J. Washington, whose prayer was quoted in part earlier in this study, stated in the same prayer the close sense of ancestral relationship commonly found in the Black prayer tradition.

> As far back as the human mind is permitted to go, we find evidences, traces of thy grace to us. Yes, from a long, long way Thou hast kept us. Thou hast befriended us. Thou hast fought for us when we were in

[9] Traditional Black spiritual.

bondage, American bondage for a number of years. We had no armies, we had no navies, we had no bombs and shots and shells, and sputniks, but we did have Thee who is an army in Thyself. And, oh, God, for a number of years our ancestors on bended knees poured out their souls unto thee through tear-blinded eyes, told Thee about themselves and about us, their children, who would follow years thereafter.[10]

Black people have never thought of themselves as an isolated generation, and nowhere is this more evident than in song and in prayer. Even without a written history of their African past, the Black people have felt a kinship with elders in the Scripture, in their native land, and in the lives of those persons who have departed this earth all about them.

Types of Imagery

The wordings of Black prayers usually called for concrete imagery rather than abstract thought. A rational mind could capture the words but lose entirely the picture. The picture was absolutely important. There was always a sense of imagery and feeling pulsating through the narrative. In a real sense their prayer language was alive and flowing with imagination.

> Language becomes closed and static by habit when the imagination fails, so that the same words are repeated without examination or critical integrity.[11]

The problem of repetition of language has been overcome in the Black prayer tradition precisely because of the involvement of one's imagination. The one who prayed lived out his or her experiences, desires, and expectations from God in such a way that the prayer became a televised experience for all who shared this event. Words and body were total tools of communication and were used to the fullest.

Several passages from the Psalms will serve as a basis of comparison with Black prayers;

> O Lord, my strength . . . my rock . . . my fortress . . . my buckler . . . my high tower (Psalm 18:1-2).

[10] Statement by Rev. C. J. Washington, Richmond, Virginia, January 1, 1974.
[11] Philip Wheelwright, *Metaphor and Reality* (Bloomington, Ind.: Indiana University Press, 1962), p. 37. Copyright © 1962 by Indiana University Press. Reprinted by permission of the publisher.

For this shall every one that is godly pray unto thee in a time when thou mayest be found: surely in the floods of great waters they shall not come nigh unto him.

Thou art my hiding place; thou shalt preserve me from trouble, thou shalt compass me about with songs of deliverance.

I will instruct thee and teach thee in the way which thou shalt go: I will guide thee with mine eye (Psalm 32:6-8).

O Lord my God, I cried unto thee, and thou hast healed me. O Lord, thou hast brought up my soul from the grave: thou hast kept me alive, that I should not go down to the pit (Psalm 30:2-3).

The following prayer, typical of style and content, was prayed by a deacon during a camp meeting held in South Nashville, Tennessee, in the summer of 1928. It is full of images which describe divine activity in behalf of the seeker.

Almighty! and all wise God our heavenly Father! 'tis once more and again that a few of your beloved children are gathered together to call upon your holy name. We bow at your foot-stool, Master, to thank you for our spared lives. We thank you that we were able to get up this morning clothed in our right mind. For Master, since we met here, many have been snatched out of the land of the living and hurled into eternity. But through your goodness and mercy we have been spared to assemble ourselves here once more to call upon a Captain who has never lost a battle. Oh, throw round us your strong arms of protection. Bind us together in love and union. Build us up where we are torn down and strengthen us where we are weak. Oh, Lord! Oh, Lord! take the lead of our minds, place them on heaven and heavenly divine things. Oh, God, our Captain and King! search our hearts and if you find anything there contrary to your divine will just move it from us, Master, as far as the east is from the west. Now Lord, you know our hearts, you know our heart's desire. You know our down-setting and you know our up-rising. Lord, you know all about us because you made us. Lord! Lord! One more kind favor I ask of you. Remember the man that is to stand in the gateway and proclaim your Holy Word. Oh, stand by him. Strengthen him where he is weak and build him up where he is torn down. Oh, let him down into the deep treasures of your word.

And now, oh, Lord, when this humble servant is done down here in this low land of sorrow: done sitting down and getting up: done being called everything but a child of God; oh, when I am done, done, done, and this old world can afford me a home no longer, right soon in the morning, Lord, right soon in the morning, meet me down at the River of Jordan, bid the waters to be still, tuck my little soul away in that snow-white chariot, and bear it away over yonder in the third heaven where every day will be a

Sunday and my sorrows of this old world will have an end, is my prayer for Christ my Redeemer's sake and amen and thank God.[12]

Several metaphors in this prayer show similarity with Old Testament thought. The psalmist says, "Exalt ye the Lord our God, and worship at his footstool; for he is holy" (Psalm 99:5). The deacon prays, "We bow at your foot-stool." The prophet says, "Thou wilt keep him in perfect peace, whose mind is stayed on thee . . ." (Isaiah 26:3). The deacon prays, "O Lord! Take the lead of our minds, place them on heaven and heavenly divine things." "Throw round us your strong arm of protection" is generally an allusion to God's protective care as extended to the people of Israel in their pilgrimage from Egypt to Canaan.

The prayer asked God to "strengthen him where he is weak and build him up where he is torn down." It was believed that God could provide instant illumination, could give instant wisdom, and could instantly place his word in his servant's mouth! This is why God was asked to "search our hearts." "Search me, O God, and know my heart: try me, and know my thoughts: And see if there be any wicked way in me, and lead me in the way everlasting" (Psalm 139:23-25).

The expression of utter humility and dependency on God was standard. God was the one who in death made the Jordan behave. A typical phrase was, "right soon in the morning, Lord, right soon in the morning, meet me down at the River of Jordan, bid the waters to be still, tuck my little soul away in that snow-white chariot, and bear it away over yonder in the third heaven. . . ." [13] Jordan was symbolically the "last river to cross." And only God could calm her tides and make her waves behave.

Of note, also, was the fact that the believer desired to cross Jordan in the morning. Here again the import of language suggested a new day and a new state of being. So strong was the sense of "the morning" in Black prayers, that one would often hear a believer opening his prayer with "this morning, our Father in Heaven," and the actual hour would be afternoon or night.

From rising in the morning until the end of the day, the Black prayer saw the hand of God. From the beginning of their spiritual

---

[12] Langston Hughes and Arna Bontemps, eds., *The Book of Negro Folklore* (New York: Dodd, Mead and Company, 1958), pp. 256-257.

[13] *Ibid.*, p. 257.

pilgrimage, when their souls were saved, until they came down to the Jordan River, they saw the hand of God. God was always moving, acting, protecting, and keeping his own. He was a "Rock," a "Bridge," a "Shelter," a "mighty Tower." One's imagination was always free to express the power of God as He worked among his people.

We also noted the poetic quality of this style of prayer. This quality was invaluable in keeping prayer experience alive. The tensive problems of life were better expressed in a language full of imagination. The result was a prayer experience that provided solutions to life's grave problems, by proclaiming affirmations of truth in poetic terms.

> Now what is it for language to be alive? In all organic life there is a ceaseless but varying struggle between opposite forces, and without such struggle the organism would go dead. . . . In man the basic organic strife shows itself in various tensions, of which he may be unconscious or at most only partly conscious—the tension between self and other persons, between self and physical environment, between love and antagonism, between one's impulses and the decisions of rational thought, between the life-urge and the dark fascination of death. As man gropes to express his complex nature and his sense of the complex world, he seeks or creates representational and expressive forms, the two adjectives standing for complementary aspects of a single endeavor which shall give some hint, always finally insufficient, of the turbulent moods within and the turbulent world of qualities and forces, promises and threats, outside him. . . .
>
> Thus language that strives toward adequacy—as opposed to signs and words of practical intent or of mere habit—is characteristically tensive to some degree and in some manner or other. This is true whether the language consists of gestures, drawings, musical compositions or (what offers by far the largest possibilities of development) verbal language consisting of words, idioms, and syntax. A gesture in the worship of a tutelary daemon, or a phrase of the Lord's prayer, is originally and properly alive and tensive.[14]

The deacon's prayer revealed this inner need to make meaning of the tensions he found in life. He was able to get up from his bed clothed anew in his right mind. Others had been cut off from the land of the living, but his life had been spared. He knew he was alive only through the strong arm of God's protection. His poetic language expressed all of these feelings in his soul.

[14] Wheelwright, op. cit., pp. 45-47.

Poetic language generally, by reason of its openness, tends towards semantic plenitude rather than toward a cautious semantic economy. The power of speaking by indirection and by evoking larger, more universal meanings than the same utterance taken in its literal sense would warrant, is one species of semantic plenitude.[15]

We saw how the deacon's prayer pointed beyond himself. He wanted his words to point to a source of Being beyond this life. In his prayer language, he wanted his hearers to know that his life had universal meaning, and his destination was "the third heaven where every day [would] be a Sunday and [his] sorrows of this old world [would] have an end."

Linkage to Prophetic Tradition

Noteworthy was the fact that Black people never identified fully with the priestly, kingly, or Deuteronomic traditions of Old Testament thought. These traditions usually meant maintaining the status quo. They meant subjecting their lives to legalisms that were often cold and indifferent, even negating their concern for freedom. Black people identified with the prophetic tradition. Here strong, spirit-filled men cried out against sin, condemned the rulers and kings where needed, built the walls of Zion, and identified with the people's struggle for deliverance. In the prayers of Black people, the preacher was generally a kind of prophet who was "to stand in the gateway and proclaim [God's] Holy Word." He was the one who "stood in the shoes of John." He, therefore, needed to be "let . . . down into the deep treasures of [God's] word" so that he might bring up both old and new.

The intense relationship in the black church between the preacher and the congregation is dependent upon the congregation being a community, a sacred family, in which the preacher is the leader and the head of the community. This relationship is similar to that of the elder in a West African village extended family compound. The elder is understood to have superior contact with the Unknown, but his relationship to it is manifested through his relationship with his people.

If we look at the published autobiographies of black churchmen whose careers began before the Civil War, we find men who are seen by their communities as having special grace manifested by their deep knowledge of the people's need. Such clergymen functioned as community

[15] *Ibid.,* p. 57.

leaders, political directors, healers and inspirers, physicians, and lawyers. The leaders of major slave revolts, such as Nat Turner, were usually such men. . . .

Their power is not derived from some legal or constitutional authority but from the traditional respect afforded elders because they are believed to act not out of selfish self-seeking motives, but out of their deep contact with the soul of the congregation and the community. The cries of "Amen," "Halleluja," "Tell it to them, Preacher," and the like that punctuate the sermon of the black preacher are in effect affirmations that he is in tune with the soul of the community.[16]

Theological Influences from the New Testament

The New Testament provided the slave with the reality of three forces, among others, that had far-reaching impact. The slave found in the person of Jesus, a savior, a friend, and fellow sufferer at the hands of the unjust oppressor, who would do anything but fail. The church became a new community whose fellowship was found with sisters and brothers in a log cabin, a field, or a plantation chapel. Here the slaves could shout, tune up, and talk with Jesus on the telephone in his bosom. The New Testament also assured them of the reality of eternal life. They knew the burdens down here would soon be dropped for the joys over there.

The Almighty Name of Jesus

> I know Jesus am a *medicine-man,*
> I know Jesus kin understan';
> I know Jesus am a bottle uv gold,
> He takes jes' one bottle ter cure a
> sin-sick soul.[17]

These words, uttered years ago by an old woman in a revival meeting, carried more meaning than meets the eye. A basic expression among Black people was "Jesus never fails" or "Christ is the answer." He was the answer to all of life's needs, frustrations, and problems. Doctrines about his theological nature were subordinate to his pragmatic power in life. He was experienced as a savior and a friend. There was no human condition that Jesus could not meet!

The Black people's traditional conditioning from West African

[16] Rawick, *op. cit.,* vol. 1, pp. 38-39.
[17] Newbell Niles Puckett, *Folk Beliefs of the Southern Negro* (Chapel Hill, N.C.: The University of North Carolina Press, 1926), p. 567.

religions made them totally receptive to the person of Jesus. In the Yoruba religion there is a god called Elegba. "He brings divinity down to earth, ... acts as messenger of the other gods, and announces death. He delivers sacrifices to Olorun, the Sky God," and he determines in great measure the destinies of people's lives according to their deeds.[18] In a word, he is the messenger of the gods who relates them to humans. The role of divine mediator was not new to Black belief.

With such a background of this and similar African deities, it was not hard for Black people to assign to Jesus literal powers. He "came in my sick room." He "cooled scorching fever and calmed troubled minds." He was a "heart fixer and mind regulator." He was a "lawyer in the courtroom, doctor in the sick room, friend to the friendless, husband to the widow, mother to the motherless, and father to the fatherless." He saved from sin, had power over the "devil," and guided his children with his eye. All these basic deeds were continually attributed to him in prayer.

Following is a description of an elderly slave woman. Her prayer captures the importance of the person of Jesus.

Inasmuch as Ye Have Done It

Aunt Jane's Prayer

She was an old Negro woman, apparently of the lowest type. Over the white wool on her head was tied a dingy handkerchief. Her dress was two cotton waists put on one over the other so that the holes and rents came in different places. The skirt was a gift from Northern barrels, as was the white apron, her only bit of Sunday finery. The home she had left that Sunday morning was not more than twelve feet square—a low, clapboarded shed with a square hole for a window closed by a wooden shutter. The chimney was of sticks, daubed with clay. The furniture was a bunk filled with pine needles and covered with pieces of carpet and quilt, a pail, and a number of empty tin meat cans, and a saucepan through whose holes she had drawn rags to stop them up. Her breakfast had been "hominy, dry so"; that is, without the little salt-pork fat or skim milk which constituted her luxuries.

She had walked a mile and a half to church, curtsied as she entered, sat down among others nearly as poor as herself, and listened to the chapter read. The leader of the meeting asked her to pray and she knelt down.

The editor interjects, "I reproduce the prayer as nearly as I can recollect it, changing some of the idioms to make it intelligible."

[18] Rawick, *op. cit.,* vol. 1, p. 47.

"Dear Massa Jesus, we all uns beg Ooner [you] come make us a call dis yere day. We is nutting but poor Etiopian women and people ain't tink much 'bout we. We ain't trust any of dem great high people for come to we church, but do' you is de one great Massa, great too much dan Massa Linkum, you ain't shame to care for we African people.

"Come to we, dear Massa Jesus. De sun, he hot too much, de road am dat long and boggy [sandy] and we ain't got no buggy for send and fetch Ooner. But Massa, you 'member how you walked dat hard walk up Calvary and ain't weary but tink about we all dat way. We know you ain't weary for to come to we. We pick out de torns, de prickles, de brier, de back-slidin' and de quarrel and de sin out of you path so dey shan't hurt Ooner pierce feet no more.

"Come to we, dear Massa Jesus. We all uns ain't got no good cool water for give you when you thirsty. You know, Massa, de drought so long, and de well so low, ain't nutting but mud to drink. But we gwine to take de 'munion cup and fill it wid de tear of repentance, and love clean out of we heart. Dat all we hab to gib you, good Massa.

"An' Massa Jesus, you say you gwine stand to de door and knock. But you ain't gwine stand at we door, Massa, and knock. We set de door plum open for you and watch up de road for see you.

"Sisters," turning to them, "what for you all ain't open de door so Massa know He welcome?"

One woman rose quietly from her knees and set the church door wide open.

"Come, Massa Jesus, come! We know you is near, we heart is all just tremble, tremble, we so glad for hab you here. And Massa, we church ain't good nuff for you to sit down in, but stop by de door just one minute, dear Massa Jesus, and whisper one word to we heart—one good word—we do listen—Massa—"

And there was silence, none moved, none spoke, and in the stillness I, for one, knew that the Lord, so earnestly called, had whispered "one good word" to my heart.[19]

Just the name "Jesus" had dynamic spiritual meaning. At times, it appeared that calling his name was a throwback to magic, superstition, or some strange belief that salvation was imparted by simply calling the name.

Uh Jesus, we know all power is in thy hand, Uh Jesus! Uh Jesus! We need you right now, Uh Jesus, I know you have heard me pray in days that's past and gone. Don't turn a deaf ear to thy servant's prayer right now, Uh Jesus, Uh Jesus![20]

[19] See Untitled Reports, Howard University Library, Washington, D.C., M248–M96. February, 1974. Used by permission of Hampton Institute Press.
[20] Traditional Black prayer lines.

One can just feel the yearning desire for Jesus to break through and make himself known.

> Lord Jesus, as you are making your heavenly circuit today, O won't you please come by here; we can't do nothing till you come. We don't just want you to stop by here, but we want you to stop by the hospital. . . . [the prayer sometimes calls the names of specific persons, including also the jails and homes for elderly, etc.][21]
> We want you, Lord Jesus, to take us out of self today; let us feel your spirit moving from heart to heart and breast to breast. If you find anything like sin, cast it in the sea of forgetfulness where it will never rise up to shame us in this world nor condemn us before the judgment bar of our God.[22]

There appeared to be no difference between Jesus, Father, God, or Holy Spirit. All of these proper names for God were used interchangeably in prayer language. Thus, Jesus was the one who spoke the world into creation. He was the power behind the church. He was the Spirit who breathed on the church, who filled the believer with the Holy Ghost. He alone was the soon-coming King. He was not thought of as a being locked in transcendent glory, aloof from the needs of his people. On the contrary, he was the One who was always there sticking closer than a brother. Jesus, the prayer says, "was all one needs!"

The Security of the Church

Jesus said in Scripture, "Where two or three are gathered in my name, there am I in the midst of them" (Matthew 18:20). This statement had literal meaning for the slave. Church was therefore not a building with a high steeple, painted white, located on top of a hill. Church for the Black slave was a spiritual happening that took place whenever the saints got together in Jesus' name. This place could be a log cabin, a praise house, a cornfield, or some clearing way down in the valley. Church in the Black prayer tradition was a spiritual presence felt by all persons in attendance, that caused each person to feel oneself in the presence of God. Some familiar prayer lines, commonly heard in the Black church follow:

> We thank Thee, O God our Father, that when we "woke up this morning, we had a mind to make our way on up to Zion where we could pick and choose our own praying ground. . . ."

[21] Traditional Black prayer lines.
[22] Traditional Black prayer lines.

We heard you say in your word, Lawd Jesus, that where two or three are gathered together in your name, touching and agreeing on the same thing, you would be right there in the midst of them. We are calling on you, Lawd, knowing you will not fail us now.

We thank thee for the church founded on thy Word. For we know that the gates of Hell shall not prevail against thy church.

We gather here today, a few of your handmade believing servants, calling on a Captain who never lost a battle.[23]

These common expressions reflect the strong sense of security the Black person has traditionally found in the church. The church was a "Noah's Ark" that shielded one's life from the rain. It was the "old ship of Zion" fully capable of sailing the seas of life. Again it was the "Gospel Train" whose engineer was Jesus and whose ticket was purchased by having faith in Jesus as Savior of the world. To write off the feelings and emotions Black people found in church as the outburst of illiterate people would be acting naively. In church everyone could really be somebody. One could participate in the meeting as he or she was moved by the spirit to do so. In a log chapel or a clapboard church building, the Black slaves found a way to develop indigenous leadership and to build a corporate fellowship. In church their souls found expression in community and family ancestry. Here, contact with God and fellowship one with another were renewed as often as the experience in worship permitted.

Going to church for Black people meant fellowshipping in God's presence in some special way. A sense of expectancy developed as one anticipated just what might happen in church on that particular day. Rev. Freeman Johnson caught this sense of expectancy when he prayed a spontaneous prayer at the revival in Lynchburg, Virginia, in 1962:

Lord God, we know you are everywhere, but in your house we expect to find you in a special way. In your house we expect you to make yourself real to us.[24]

Preparation for Sunday's worship has traditionally begun on Saturday in Black homes. Mothers would cook Sunday's meals on Saturday. The family would all take Saturday night baths. Sunday clothes were laid out and shoes were shined. Sunday morning meant eating a full breakfast and sharing a moment of prayer around the

[23] Traditional Black prayer lines.
[24] Prayer by Rev. Freeman Johnson, at Court Street Baptist Church, Lynchburg, Virginia, October, 1962.

table. All of these acts inevitably led up to the big moment of worship in church. Here all were expected to sing their songs to God. People could pray as they felt led. No one could reasonably escape the sense of being in church where God was at work in some special way.

The Hope of Eternal Life

The following closing statements to prayers were taken at random from a city-wide revival.

> Finally, Lord, when I'm done with the troubles of this ol' world, when I've gone in my room to come out no more, when my tongue cleaves to the roof of my mouth and my eyelids fall to rise no more, take me home to be with thee, where Job declared, "the wicked shall cease from troubling and my weary soul shall be at rest. . . ." Amen and Thank God.
>
> Lord, you said in your Word that if I own you down here, you would own me over there. Help me, Lord, to live so that when I'm through down here, I'll have a place over there, among the redeemed and blest of God, where every day will be Sunday and Sabbath will have no end.
>
> Lord, when this ol' world can afford us a home no longer, when we have to lay down our swords and spears and study war no more, we want to hear your welcoming voice, saying, "Well done! Well done! Thou good and faithful servant, thou hast been faithful over a few things; come up higher, and I will make you ruler over many" is thy servant's prayer for Christ's sake. And Amen and Thank God.[25]

Once the believer was on board the gospel train, his final destination was Glory Land. Black people did not question, by and large, the question of a person's ongoing existence beyond this world. In their prayers they traveled the wings of words to Beulah Land time after time. They were told in prayers that they have "a Heaven to see and a Hell to shun."

Heaven, in this tradition, was more than a figment of the imagination. It was really more than the yearning of souls seeking to be free! Heaven was that perfect place, experienced in imperfect communion down here. Heaven was that place where one's soul desired to be. Here one was a citizen of the kingdom of God, sojourning in a strange land. Therefore, one's soul and spirit reached out for the other world. The wings of prayer and the force of the word transported the mind to it! Thus the Black people prayed, without

[25] Traditional Black prayer lines, heard in a city-wide revival, Baltimore, Maryland, January, 1974.

apology, wanting to go to heaven when they died, and making a kind of heavenly interior living space while still here.

Theological Influences of the Prayer Event Itself

The event of prayer in the Black religious community was one involving the person who prayed, the words used, and the total response of the congregation. As one prayed, he or she led the entire congregation to the throne of grace. In this exalted act one ministered to the congregation. Things that could not otherwise be said and accepted by the community were received in the hour of prayer. Therefore, it was usually felt that something should happen when the event of prayer took place.

The Person

The person who prayed in the Black prayer tradition was always doing three things. First, one was literally talking with God. Such a person was convinced the Spirit was telling him or her what to say. Secondly, one was talking with oneself. A person's own problems, frustrations, yearnings, and expectations came through in the moment of prayer. Thirdly, one was talking with those persons who joined with one in the act of worship. The act of prayer was always a supreme moment when the person's life was literally shared in an act of divine communication.

Prayer, therefore, was an event in the Black congregation. It was that moment when the Spirit of God possessed the person who prayed. Prayer in this tradition was more than a ritual or literary composition. Prayer was a person talking to the Father in Jesus' name. The force of imagery took over, and Jesus, the anthropomorphic God-man, came riding on in the hearts of his people, building lives up where they were torn down, and fixing broken hearts. The Savior was always "a-listening to hear somebody pray." The one at prayer became robed with a spiritual dimension. It was no longer a person who spoke, but it was the Spirit of God speaking through that person.

The writer observed the African heritage for this tradition in two trips to West Africa. In Nigeria and Ghana, Africans would cover their bodies with colorful masks and perform dances. Through these rituals, they no longer acted as themselves, but as the beings or spirits possessing them. The writer was told that social standards were maintained and preserved through this method of communicating certain basic folkways and beliefs from persons in another state of being.

> When an African dons a mask and performs certain dances or sings about people or events, he is no longer acting as a person but as a being or spirit. In this role he often has freedom for comments on social relations and for actions that, if made unmasked, would produce social friction or hostilities.[26]

The writer checked with the deacons of New Shiloh Baptist Church about this general folk belief of being possessed by the Spirit of God while praying. One of the deacons asked, "Reverend, do you feel it is all right for one to read his prayers?" Knowing the basic Black prayer tradition, it was obvious that this question was charged with meaning. Yet one could not deny what appeared to be the truth. The answer given was "Yes!" In fact, such a practice could really increase the power of prayer by sharpening one's thoughts and polishing one's words. However, the majority of the men felt that spontaneous prayer that comes gushing up from the soul was a vivid sign that God was truly with one in prayer. This sacred spell was broken by a manuscript. God was not on the paper; he was only in the heart. The minority agreed that many of our prayers are repetitious and that preplanned thought was most beneficial. The minority, however, did not have gusto or enthusiasm in their beliefs, as did the majority.

The fact is, when the average Black person prays in church, he or she dons the robe of the spiritual. "The knee is bent and body bowed," even though a person may actually be standing! One is "an empty pitcher before a full fountain, waiting to be filled!" One is "God's humble servant, whom the Lord has heard many times before, but realizes that prayer is much desired to be made again!" One is a "poor wretched creature of a moment, making his peace, calling and election sure!" One comes to God in gratitude for "lengthening out the brickly threads of his unprofitable life, and bidding his golden moments to run on a little while longer." A person comes as one not knowing how to pray, but believing that the Spirit of God will give one the word and power of prayer. Thus one prays. One may rub

---

[26] Simon and Phoebe Ottenberg, eds., *Cultures and Societies of Africa* (New York: Random House, Inc., 1960), p. 68.

his or her hands together or clasp them. One may actually kneel or walk about while praying. Almost always, one will let the voice rise in emotional crescendo as the power of the prayer mounts. Such behavior at prayer is acceptable as long as one prays sincerely. In this moment a person is no longer oneself but is totally in conversation with God.

The Word

The word of prayer must always ring a bell, paint an image, drive home a message, and point the listener to God. A woman was heard praying the following prayer in a revival meeting in Baltimore, Maryland.

> O God, our help in ages past, our hope for years to come, Thou art our shelter in the stormy blast, and our eternal home.
> O God, my Father, I thank you tonight for your loving kindness and your tender mercies. 'Thank you, Holy Father, for your blessed Word, a lamp unto our feet and a light along our pathway. We want to thank you for your Word that brought salvation. I want to thank you tonight, Lord God, that you included me a long time ago. You shed your blood on Calvary's cross, and gave your life that I might live! I want to thank you for it. You blest and enabled me to see Thee out of thine Word. I thank Thee for giving thine manservant wisdom and power from his lips, for we have heard the Gospel tonight. O God, my Father, let your spirit ride, that the Word may find its place in the hearts of men and women, that it might bring forth fruit unto Thee. O God, let our coming not be in vain. Somebody needs you right now. O God, my Father, would that you would convict and convert sinners that they might cry out, "What must I do to be saved?" O God, let them not be satisfied until they've yielded their lives to Thee. Then, my Father, when I've gone that last mile of the way, I want to be able to say, "I've fought a good fight, I have finished my course, I have kept the faith." I want to hear thy welcoming voice saying, "Enter into the joy of thy Master," Amen.

This prayer was prayed after the sermon in a revival. Notice how the prayer exhorted the congregation on the basis of personal experience with God. The one who prayed was convinced she was included in God's elect, and she rejoiced for having heard God's Word just preached. This strength was used to challenge those not in the fold to receive what she now had experienced by being convicted and converted. Again we see how the robe of prayer equips one to speak with drive and authority to the community.

This research has not produced any evidence of Black people being critical of the words of prayer. Words may be grammatically broken; statements at times may be very personal, but the event itself lifts the person who prays on the wings of the Spirit.

A man in a church in Washington, D.C., when called on to pray, said, "O Lord, I really don't know why they called on me to pray. I guess they know you and me are on speaking terms, and that we know how to talk to one another." [27] Knowing how to pray "the word" in the Black church was a pearl of great price. Talking to God meant the gradual crescendo of voice, emotion, word, and spirit. When these faculties were smoothly harmonized, the total personality was fully involved.

Because the person and the word blended so closely together in this tradition, some persons gained great popularity as being powerful in prayer. This illustrative and interesting account comes from slave narratives.

> "The old white woman that owned the place was rich—big rich. She been complaining about the noise—singing and preaching. She called him Praying Jim Jesus till he got to be called that around. He prayed in the field. She said he disturbed her. Mama said one of the Ku Klux she knowed been raised up there close to Master Barton's but papa said he didn't know one of them that beat on him." [28]

While the above slave's prayers were no doubt sincere, and his popularity was wide, others whose motives may have been mixed have become popular at prayer.

Ministers attending the National Baptist Convention, U.S.A., Inc., have looked forward for someone to pray who could really stir up the masses, especially at certain points during the session. There was a popular story in ministerial circles that the late D. V. Jemison, president of the National Baptist Convention, Inc., was literally prayed into office by J. W. Tate, a minister who gained great prominence as having power to pray. Samuel McKinney gave an eyewitness report of the incident:

> I was right there, with my father. The spirit was high. They put Tate up to pray, and he "turned the convention out." After his prayer, Dr. Jemison was in. I heard Rev. Tate state after the session, when someone asked him,

[27] Statement reported by William A. Jones, Jr., clergyman, in personal interview, Rochester, New York, July, 1974.

[28] Rawick, *op. cit.,* vol. 10, part 6, p. 224.

"Why did you pray like that?" Ol' man Tate said, "Well, when I am at home, I pray to God; but when I am in conventions, I pray to the folk."[29]

One can surmise that prayers are offered for showmanship on many occasions. A deacon in a Baptist church in Newark, New Jersey, said in his prayer, "Lord, I want to thank you that when I got up this morning and came to church, my name was not on the bulletin sick list, and when I read the obituary column in the paper, my name was not on the death list."[30] Statements like this are often designed as showmanship and received by some persons as entertainment. For others, it is a moment of sincere prayer.

In the Black church, it has been an accepted practice to call on certain men or women to pray when the spirit of worship was sluggish. It has been popularly believed that certain persons had the gift of prayer, the word of prayer, and things would happen spiritually when they prayed.

The Congregation

Congregational participation in prayer was a must. There must be witnessing in responsive words and mournful sounds. The writer's own Alabama background witnessed to this fact. As the leader in prayer would offer up petitions to God, someone moved by the spirit of God would lead a one line song-chant, such as:

> Have mercy—have mercy, Lord—Mmmm
> Have mercy, have mercy now!

or

> Come, Holy Spirit,
> We sure do need you now—Mmmm

again

> It's a mighty long journey,
> But I'm on my way—Mmmm
> It is a mighty long journey
> But I'm on my way. . . .

These prayerful congregational moans lend themselves to any one- or

[29] Statement by Samuel Berry McKinney, clergyman, personal interview, Rochester, New York, July, 1974.

[30] Statement by William A. Jones, Jr., clergyman, personal interview, Baltimore, Maryland, August 24, 1974.

two-line thoughts that strike the believer in worship. The apparent purpose is to create a sense of worship and divine movement in the congregation. The modern version of this old-time moaning practice is the playing of soft organ music as a meditative background to prayer.

The verbal response, however, remains and is commonly accepted. The congregation responds with shouts of "Amen," "Yes, Lord," "Oh, yes," "Help us, Lord" or "Hear us, Lord," "Help him to pray, church." Others simply bow their heads and nod them up and down in an outward consent to the message of prayer. The event of prayer develops its full intensity when the leader and the congregation find a oneness in thought, emotion, rhythm, and spirit. The church is on the main line now, and the believer can tell God what he wants!

James Baldwin described the congregational spirit at work. Writing of his own storefront church experience while growing up in Harlem, he gave this reflection:

> The church was very exciting. It took a long time for me to disengage myself from this excitement, and on the blindest, most visceral level, I never really have, and never will. There is no music like that music, no drama like the drama of the saints rejoicing, the sinners moaning, the tambourines racing, and all those voices coming together and crying holy unto the Lord. There is still, for me, no pathos quite like the pathos of those multicolored, worn, somehow triumphant and transfigured faces, speaking from the depths of a visible, tangible, continuing despair of the goodness of the Lord. I have never seen anything to equal the fire and excitement that sometimes, without warning, fill a church, causing the church, as Leadbelly and so many others have testified, to "rock." Nothing that has happened to me since equals the power and the glory that I sometimes felt when, in the middle of a sermon, I knew that I was somehow, by some miracle, really carrying, as they said, "the Word"— when the church and I were one. Their pain and their joy were mine, and mine were theirs—they surrendered their pain and joy to me, I surrendered mine to them—and their cries of "Amen!" and "Hallelujah!" and "Yes, Lord!" and "Praise His name!" and "Preach it, brother!" sustained and whipped on my solos until we all became equal, wringing wet, singing and dancing, in anguish and rejoicing, at the foot of the altar.[31]

Baldwin described in strong, vivid language his boyhood experience in a Harlem storefront congregation. The sense of oneness

---

[31] James Baldwin, *The Fire Next Time* (New York: The Dial Press, 1963), pp. 47-48. Copyright © 1963 by James Baldwin. Reprinted by permission of The Dial Press.

and mutually sharing one another's burdens come through in his reported experience.

In like manner, the one who prayed was in effect sharing with the congregation God's Word in prayer. Of course every congregation did not become as involved as the preceding congregational experience. Many congregations would not have the tambourines, the dance, and the outward sense of rejoicing. But whenever the freely expressive prayer was expected and practiced, some sense of involved oneness had to happen for the prayer to be truly effective.

The Person and Place of the Devil

Black people seem to have the uncanny sense of visualizing and making real. There is a strong tendency to pay attention to that personal cosmic being commonly called the devil. Attempts are made to control him through exorcising and through fighting and subduing him in Jesus' name.

The devil emerged in this study as the chief enemy of men and women and one who worked also against the program of God. He was sometimes seen as having a pitchfork and red suit and working in a fiery pit! He exercised final and absolute control over the wicked. He punished the living on earth.

No doubt much of the imagery of the devil, coming through prayers of Black people, was deliberately taught them by White masters and preachers as another way of controlling the slave's mind to accept their state of submission.

An Alabama witness tells of a woman convert's vision:

> Ah wuz tu'k by a strand uv my hair and shuck over hell, and all de hair broke and Ah wuz about to fall in hell. Ah looked down and there Ah see'd a black man, and Ah know'd dat was de debul, and Ah sed, "Lawd, hab mussy!" And jes' as dat-ah black man wuz tryin' ter ketch me on his pitchfork, Ah see'd a littl' w'ite man and Ah know'd dat wuz Jesus, and Ah sed, "Sabe me, Lawd!" And dat littl' w'ite man tu'k and kicked dat black man in de haid and he fell back in hell, and dat w'ite man tu'k me in His arms, and Ah know Ah's got de' ligion, caze Ah felt lak Ah nebber felt befo'![32]

We see the stereotype of a White savior and a Black devil. We also see the self-condemnation suffered by Black people en masse during the long night of mental and physical oppression.

[32] Puckett, *op. cit.*, pp. 540-541.

At times the devil was portrayed in Ku Klux Klan imagery. Miss Irene Robertson told this experience:

> They didn't have the Ku Klux but it was bout like what they had. They wore caps shine de coons eye and red caps and red garments. Red symbolize blood reason they wore red. They broke up our preaching. Some folks got killed. Some was old, some young—old devlish ones. They was like a drove of varments. I guess you be scared. They run the colored folks away from church a lot of times. That was about equalization after the freedom. That was the cause of that.[33]

There were various images of Satan. Many Black straw bosses were as mean, if not meaner than, their White counterparts. In some minds, the Black man himself became a type of Satan. More prevalent, however, was the devil in a red suit and with a pitchfork who was addressed as Captain Satan, no doubt a counterpart of the White slave system.

Getting religion would really mean outwitting and outrunning the devil.

> Old Satan is a liar an' conjurer, too,
> An' if you don't mind out, he'll conjure you.
> Ole Satan lak a snake in the grass,
> Always in some Christian's path. . . .

or

> If you don't mind out, he'll get you at las'.[34]

The Black person was therefore on the alert, always seeking to outrun and outwit the devil. The greatest tool for doing this was praying, in the name of Jesus. A believer was convinced that any obstacle could be surmounted through the power of Jesus Christ. These familiar lines were prayed over and over again:

> Lord, you snatched my soul from the gates of hell, you put a new song in my heart and a new word in my mouth, you gave me a mind to do right and a mind to pray right.

Again he prayed:

> I want to thank you, Lord Jesus, that when I had no eye to pity me, no hand to save me, you snatched my soul from hell and told me that if I

[33] Rawick, op. cit., vol. 10, part 6, p. 77.
[34] Traditional Black prayer lines.

would go, you would go with me, open my mouth and you would speak for me.[35]

Satan was always that force working against the good of people. He opposed the program of God. He vexed the mind and spirit of a person. He was a spiritual power and was present everywhere, always seeking to subdue and conjure the lives of people.

The one source of power to wage war on the devil was the name of Jesus. Imaginary or real, many a battle has been fought and won, using Jesus' name in prayer. A few prayer illustrations follow:

We gather here tonight to declare war on Satan and to put an end to the powers of sin.

Satan, God rebuke you, and we declare you to be a liar through the blood of Jesus Christ.

We know, oh, Lord, that Satan is busy going to and fro in the streets of the city, devouring whom he may, but we thank God for the victory we have over Satan right now.

We thank you, Lord, that you got up one morning from the grave and declared your power over sin, death, and hell, and declared, "Whosoever will, let him come." We thank you for it.[36]

The code language for victory over sin and Satan was always the same. It was expressed in statements that follow:

Children, I feel better now.
I can now run on a little while longer.
Thank God, I got my blessing.
Yes! Yes! Yes! [Sometimes just spoken and again sung in a chant] Yes! Yes! Yes![37]

All of this brings to mind a model prayer, uttered by the venerable W. L. Ransome, who closed a recent session of the annual Hampton Ministers' Conference, where more than eight hundred ministers gathered in a traditional preaching and prayer renewal service.

Almighty God, we thank thee for the hours we have spent on this campus. Every now and then when the way seems dark, you give us a little sample of what is better further along. We have been encouraged this week by the fact that what we have received is a sample of that which is waiting for those who hold out and prove faithful to the end. We are like the ox

[35] Traditional Black prayer lines.
[36] Traditional Black prayer lines, expressed by deacons in a city-wide revival, Baltimore, January, 1974.
[37] Traditional Black responses to prayer.

who is pulling the load up the hill, and about to give out; when the driver gets out of the ox cart and carries a little food up the hill—and the oxen know the food is up there, by faith they pull harder. We are gonna pull harder now. We are gonna cut more deeply. We are gonna believe more firmly. We are gonna hold more assuredly, because one thing you told Peter, "that the gates of hell will not prevail against the church."

Help us to go back now. When Samson wanted to burn down the wheat fields of the Philistines, he got a hundred or so foxes and tied their tails together. He struck one match and lighted all those fiery tails and turned them loose among the wheat fields of the Philistines. When the foxes got through, the enemies of God didn't have nothing to feed on. We've been tied together here this week.

The Servant of God has lighted our hearts with the candle of Thy Word. He's turning us loose now! We're going out into the world, and we're gonna burn down hell and the kingdom of Satan in this age!

May the grace of God and the sweet communion of the Holy Spirit and the peace that passeth all understanding, abide with us until that same Jesus, who went into the first airship, manned by two pilots, ascended out of sight, and the angel said, "In like manner He's coming again."

And when He comes, when He comes, all those looking for Him by faith will be with Him and shall never separate from that Holy Church.

Where shadows never fall, calendars never bedeck the walls, funerals are never had, and parting is no more.

On the sea of glass, we will retire. Palms of victory in our hands, we will wave to Him who shall reign forevermore.[38]

The ministers' conference was closed with hands held together and voices ringing out, "God be with you until we meet again!" The ministers, like their ancestors of old, were now ready to go to the marketplace and wage war on Satan and his demonic kingdom.

The "Praise God" Factor in Prayer

The single most remarkable trait of Black prayers was the total absence of the spirit of hate, revenge, and malice, especially to the White power structure. There was a positive affirmation of life, expressed in praise. This tradition was filled with utterances of "Thank you, Jesus," "Yes, Lord," and "Through it all, the Lord been good to me." There follow some statements of slaves expressing this "praise God" concept in the everyday affairs of life.

"Thank God I'ze free as a jay bird."[39]

[38] Prayer by Dr. Ransome, Hampton Ministers' Conference, Hampton, Virginia, June 8, 1973.

[39] Rawick, op. cit., vol 10, part 5, p. 27.

"Our folks' master was William E. Johnson. Oh Lord, they was just as good to us as could be to be under slavery." [40]

"Oh Lord, I don't know what's goin' to become of us old folks. Wasn't for the Welfare, I don't know what I'd do." [41]

"Vote? Good Lord! I done more votin'. Voted for all the Presidents. Yankees wouldn't let us vote Democrat, had to vote Republican." [42]

The above statements are utterances of a life-style full of conscious and unconscious references to God. Here one uses God's name in communicating one's total experiences of life. Whatever one's experience, the person tries to see it in the hand of God at work in human affairs.

The Reverend D. E. King, a noted spiritual preacher and folklorist, gave the following examples of praise.

Sister Patsy Smith was a woman with thirteen children. Her husband abandoned her and her children. One day Sister Patsy Smith said to my mother, as she was standing out on the street shouting and praising God, "Sister King, I've run out of sugar, I've run out of coffee, pepper, and salt. I don't have any more bread, but every time I get to the end of my rope, God comes and ties another piece to that rope and lengthens it out." And there she was standing there in the street shouting and praising God. I go until I get to the end of another piece, and just about the time I think I'm about to fall off the rim of nowhere, He piles another piece on it and straightens it out.

I was with Dr. O. M. Hoover as he celebrated his twentieth anniversary last year as pastor of the Olivet Institutional Baptist Church in Cleveland, Ohio. When we went back to the hotel after church, he was riding on the back seat. He had been sick for three years. I was sitting up front with the chauffeur. I heard him cry out, and I thought he was sick! I looked back and saw the tears streaming down his cheek, and I said, "What's wrong, Hoover?" He said, "I was just sitting back here thinking about how good God is! When I pastored Mt. Zion Baptist Church in Fayetteville, Tennessee, I went to prepare myself for the ministry at American Baptist Theological Seminary. My church could only pay me twelve dollars a week. My wife was pregnant. Each Saturday when I went from Nashville to Fayetteville, I had to leave my spare tire with the service station to get enough gas to go to Fayetteville. For three years I did this. The reason I'm rejoicing is because for three years I wore my tires as clean as my hand and I never had a flat! I never had a blowout! I never had

[40] *Ibid.*, p. 1.
[41] *Ibid.*, p. 126.
[42] *Ibid.*, p. 76.

a puncture!" And he was sitting back there shouting over nearly thirty years of God's goodness.[43]

The praise and thanksgiving in Black prayers were usually related to the basic needs of life. Blacks praised God for "another day's journey," "food to eat, clothes to wear, and a shelter to retire to for rest." God was praised by the Black people for keeping them alive and preserving their health and strength and proper mental attitude. The Black person was always most grateful for God's "darling Son Jesus who hanged between the living and the dead, that we all might have a right to the tree of life."

The nature of praise to God often followed some act of divine deliverance when it was felt God's presence had lifted life from pain or sorrow.

> Once I was called to preach when I had rheumatism in my leg. My wife hobbled all along the way to church with me, telling me all the time that I should have stayed home in bed, but I told her that I must fill my hand. The rest is the Lord's. I felt awful bad when I first got to church and took my place on the stand, waiting for the congregation to gather. And then the spirit lifted me up. I forgot all about the pain and just lost sight of the world and all the things of the world. When the spirit begins to work with one, it don't have any cares for pain or anything of the world. My mind gets fixed on God and I feel a deep love, joy, and desire to be with God. We shout because we feel glad in the heart. At times I feel like I could just kiss the very feet of man, and I had rather hear the voice on the inside cry "Amen" when I do something than to have all the money in the world. We rejoice because the spirit makes us feel so good and makes us forget all worldly cares.[44]

Here the preacher was lifted from his pain on wings of the spirit. In like manner, the one who offered constant praises to God lost himself as he submitted completely to what he believed to be the will and presence of God in his life. He rejoiced in spite of the problems he faced. He rejoiced because he knew God and God knew him.

Facing Life on One's Knees

There was no room for doubt of God in this positive approach to prayer. There was a childlike faith that God would hear one when one

---

[43] From the sermon "Praising God" by Rev. D. E. King, Baltimore, Maryland, September 9, 1973.

[44] Clifton H. Johnson, ed., *God Struck Me Dead* (Philadelphia: Pilgrim Press, 1969), p. 23.

prayed. Life's battles could be fought and won on one's knees.

The three-story universe has been very strong in Black thought, but there is communication and care between the stories. God's abode was in heaven. People lived on earth. Hell and destruction were below the earth. God manifested himself on earth in the person and spirit of Christ, but his full abode was "way beyond the blue!" The Black person sang a song of prayer experience:

> Down here, Lord, waiting on you
> Can't do nothing till you come.
>
> Down here, Lord, wid my Bible
>   in ma hand—
> Can't do nothing till you come.
>
> Oh, you may be on your knees,
> Oh, you ought to ask the Holy Ghost
>   in your room.
> I'm down here, Lord, waiting on you
> Can't do nothing till you come.[45]

There was the strong element of "tarrying" found in this song. It was rooted in the belief that if one tarried long enough, with sincerity of purpose and heart, God would come and deliver one.

> Oh, you may be a motherless child
>   Haven't got a friend in de world,
> Feel like everybody done turn dere backs
>   on you.
> Oh, you ought to open your mouth and cry
> I'm down here, Lord, a-waiting on you,
> Can't do nothing till you come.[46]

When God came, he did several things. He brought deliverance from one's sins. He provided strength for facing life's problems. He provided health of body and spirit to overcome the diseases and frailties of life.

No one in modern times has lifted the dimension of facing life on one's knees as has the late Dr. Martin Luther King, Jr. When he called on his followers to face their enemies with a prayer and nonviolence based on Christian love, he was speaking to a people

---

[45] Traditional Black folk spiritual.
[46] Traditional Black folk spiritual.

whose history made them receptive to this message. Waging war on one's knees was not new! Dr. King simply gave it a new dimension.

> Talk about me just as much as you please, the more you talk I'm gonna bend my knees.[47]

Bending the knee was a necessity for Black people. They had no other collective tools with which to fight. They did have the inner strength to tell God all about their problems on their knees.

Howard Thurman gave to us this lucid example of facing life in prayer:

> When I was a student in Atlanta, a blind Negro was killed by a policeman. Feeling ran high all through the Negro community. When his funeral was held, officers of the law, fearing that it would be an occasion for some kind of uprising, came to the service but remained outside the church. In his sermon, the minister had only words of consolation to give to the family. In his prayer to God, he expressed his anger and hostility toward the white community. He could do this in a prayer without exposing the Negro community to retaliation.[48]

Obviously, the minister who prayed such a prayer knew his people were tuned to a certain spiritual dimension. Here he could get his same message over, telling God what was on the community's mind, and he could still avoid the possibility of a riot.

Many persons have argued that facing life on one's knees was resignation to one's plight. One did this, it was felt, because of lack of courage and fortitude. Not only has this attack come from the White intellectual, but it has also come from certain Blacks within the community. However, when prayer was dignified in the streets, in jails, on the steps of courthouses, and in the cause of freedom during the civil rights movements, a new respect for this ancient weapon emerged. Song and prayer merged in the language:

> Let Jesus lead you, let Jesus lead you,
> Let Jesus lead you all the way.
> All the way from earth to Heaven
> Let Jesus lead you all the way.
>
> He'll fight your battle. He'll fight your battle.
> He'll fight your battle all the way.

[47] Traditional Black folk line.
[48] Howard Thurman, *The Luminous Darkness* (New York: Harper & Row, Publishers, 1965), p. 22.

> All the way from earth to Heaven,
> He'll fight your battle all the way.[49]

The writer vividly remembers standing with a group before a jail in Lynchburg, Virginia, where some freedom fighters were held. He can hear the song now that was sung that Sunday morning.

> I'm gonna stay on bended knees,
> I'm gonna stay on bended knees,
> I'm gonna stay on bended knees
> 'til I die. . . . (*repeat*)

> I'm gonna treat everybody right,
> I'm gonna treat everybody right,
> I'm gonna treat everybody right
> 'til I die. . . . (*repeat*)[50]

Martin Luther King, Jr., knew that facing life on one's knees had been historically the only potent weapon Black people had to face life's many problems. They had no collective police powers and did not possess any organized political power. Social pressures were against them, living in a segregated way of life, and they had no collective economical power. They did, however, have a long history of taking their burdens to the Lord and leaving them there.

Dr. King used this long prayer tradition to teach Black people that the one who faces life with a prayer is not weak. On the contrary, he is exhibiting far more strength than the one supplied with man-made forces. He taught that soul power was far more effective in human redemption than physical power.

The results of this teaching found many Black persons ready and willing to take the teaching of facing life on one's knees and using it to bring freedom from unjust social laws, unjust political laws, while generating a healthier sense of community among Black people particularly and among all who shared this philosophy generally. This was the teaching that undergirded the civil rights movement under the leadership of Dr. King.

"He's Available on the Main Line"

The One who fronted and fought life's battles was always available on the main line. He alone could do what no doctor could do. He was

[49] Traditional Black folk spiritual.
[50] Traditional spiritual.

always within earshot. Therefore, one could tell Him what one wanted.

This attitude of prayer has pulled many suffering persons up from beds of illness, especially where the ailment was partly psychosomatic. "When Jesus was on the main line, nothing could fail."

The song which follows celebrates this holy assurance:

> Oh, Jesus is on the main line;
> Tell Him what you want.
>
> Jesus is on the main line;
> Tell Him what you want.
>
> Jesus is on the main line;
> Tell Him what you want,
> Call Him up and tell Him what you want.
>
> If you want religion, tell Him what
> you want.
>
> If you want the Holy Ghost, tell Him
> what you want.
>
> If you're sick and you can't get well,
> Tell Him what you want. . . .[51]

One was free to make very specific requests from God. God was asked to remove headaches, cure cataracts of the eyes, remove cancers, heal rheumatism, provide strength for feeble bodies, and calm tired nerves. The pastor in almost any Black culture church has certainly heard these words:

Rev., I'm here today by the help of the Lord . . . this ol' back of mine has been giving me trouble but I'm going on anyhow. You pray for me, Rev. . . .

Or, church members have heard in a prayer meeting:

Brothers and sisters, I didn't think I would be here tonight. I had a hard day, went home, and sat down. Ol' Satan tried to keep me from coming, but I got to thinking and praying, and I made up my mind I was coming on anyhow. Just look what a blessing I would have missed had I not come out tonight!

[51] Traditional Black folk spiritual.

It was believed that things happened when "Jesus was on the main line!" During this moment blessings occurred. An elderly minister in Norfolk, Virginia, by the name of Reverend Gray, bore witness to this point. A service of revival was going on in his church. The spirit of worship was exceedingly high. Everyone was deeply moved. In this situation Reverend Gray went down on the floor in front of the pulpit, tears flowing down his face, hands extended, telling the church, "Children, the Lord is here! He is here right now! Anyone who needs a blessing, who needs to be healed, come quickly and shake my hand; the Lord is here!"[52]

An entire thesis would not do justice to the firm belief of Black people in the immediate healing power of God. Since their native African background provided doctors and medicine men of all sorts, in some ways Jesus became the Super Doctor, the Super Personality who gathered up in himself all the instinctive and conscious beliefs of the Black people in healing faith.

The Bible provided a basis for solid theological influences in the Black prayer tradition. The Almighty God, who had always revealed genuine concern for his people, was now seen as having elected the Black people to be his chosen people in the New World. The Black people found in this chosen-people concept power to sustain their present sufferings and also power to identify with Old Testament patriarchs and elders who had walked with God before them. They could speak of God as being a "solid rock," a "battle axe," and a "mighty tower of defense." The New Testament provided them with a Savior, Jesus Christ, who was always on the main line, and the Black person could tell him what he or she wanted. This Savior, Jesus Christ, had the power to rebuke Satan and to cast out demons. The very utterance of his name brought forth spiritual power. This meant that when Black people prayed, they were no longer speaking simply for themselves or by themselves; they were now speaking in the spirit and were being used by God. In this state one could minister to the community and utter words that could not be stated otherwise. People used this power to face life on their knees and to keep in touch with Jesus, who was always on the main line.

Yes, Black people were now fortified with the Word of God, its

---

[52] Statement by Reverend Gray, in revival service, Beulah Baptist Church, Norfolk, Virginia, August, 1961.

history, its Savior, and its promise of eternal life. They had power beyond casual observation. In their minds they had become the "new Israel." The thrust of prophecy was now happening in them. They believed they could call on God and get an answer. They believed they could wage war on their knees. In doing so, they were accused of being otherworldly and failing to face reality. But these accusations would not stop their thrust. They continued their prayers and made this tradition a breeding ground for churches, social institutions, and a basis for redemptive social action.

4

Major Functions of the Black Prayer Tradition

The Black prayer tradition, rather than being an otherworldly flight, has in fact provided the setting, fervor, and visionary powers for the community outreach and action of Black people. In this setting churches have been born; ministers have been inspired; and schools have been founded.

The Old-Fashioned Prayer Meeting

Tuesday night in the Tabernacle Baptist Church, Selma, Alabama, was time for prayer meeting. D. V. Jemison, president of the National Baptist Convention, Inc., was pastor of this church. The writer was a member and shared the weekly prayer meetings with his father.

The first half hour was spent in song, prayer, and testimony. Since only a few of the "spiritual members" attended, each person usually had time to lead a song and say a prayer. The final hour was Bible study led by the minister. The Bible lesson completed, the offering

71

was received with prayer. The service closed with a special prayer for the needy, the sick, and the shut-in. This moment concretized all the acts of worship gone before and brought all present to a meaningful climax.

This basic format was typical of the Black prayer meeting, with varieties in time spent and emotional intensity involved. Since this service was rather unstructured, leaning heavily on the spirit felt, in some situations this meeting ran well into the night. In other cases it terminated after an hour or so. Its role was absolutely basic in the average Black church.

We have already seen how the Black people were sustained with prayer meetings in the midst of their slave experience. From camp to camp, log cabin to log cabin, brush arbor to brush arbor, prayer meetings were hours of communal expression far deeper than the White masters realized. In these gatherings prayer related the believers to the Ground of their being. Songs of the spirit burst forth, speaking to the basic needs of life. The freedom of open participation fostered a sense of personhood in community. Here life became meaningful and vital.

Breeding Ground for Churches

One of the first pastors of note among Black people in America founded his church with prayer. "Andrew Bryan was born a slave in 1737 at Goose Creek, South Carolina, about sixteen miles from Charleston. . . . He at first commenced by public exhortations and prayer meetings at Brampton."[1]

Here the seed of an all-important movement, the church, was about to burst forth from a traditional prayer meeting. One wonders if the White master realized its significance. Surely he did not, as he later sought to subdue this growing movement. The slaves, after Bryan and his brother Sampson were persecuted in desiring to found a new church, met for worship in a plantation barn

where they were surrounded by spies and eavesdroppers. This continued until one of the eavesdroppers, upon listening to what was going on among these communicants at Andrew Bryan's private home, heard this man of God earnestly praying for the men who had so mercilessly used him. This

[1] Carter G. Woodson, *The History of the Negro Church,* 2nd ed. (Washington, D.C.: Associated Publishers, 1921), pp. 47-48.

enlisted so much sympathy among the people kindly disposed that the chief justice of the court, before whom they had been brought, granted them permission to continue their worship of God at any time between sunrise and sunset.[2]

A similar pattern of church birth and growth is noted in the founding of the African Methodist Episcopal Church. Richard Allen, the respected founder, was born a slave in Philadelphia, Pennsylvania, to the family of Benjamin Chew. He was later sold to a planter in Dover, Delaware, where he grew to manhood. Here he came under Christian influence and was converted in 1777. A few years later he began to preach.

> Struck with the genuineness of his piety, his master permitted him to conduct prayers and to preach in his house, he himself being one of the first converts of this zealous messenger of God. Feeling after his conversion that slavery was wrong, Allen's master permitted his bondmen to obtain their freedom. Allen and his brother purchased themselves for $2,000 in the depreciated currency of the Revolutionary War.[3]

Richard Allen was now struck with a great desire to meet the needs of Black people, who had long been overlooked and were a forgotten people in basic Christian instruction. "Starting a prayer meeting in Philadelphia, he soon had 42 members."[4] Some months later Richard Allen, Absalom Jones, and William White were pulled off their knees as they prayed in the white St. George Methodist Episcopal Church in Philadelphia, and immediately they arose and withdrew from the church. Allen and Jones as a result formed what was the beginning of the independent Free African Society.[5]

After the days of slavery, when Black people migrated en masse to the urban North, the house-to-house prayer meetings provided the welcome mat from one community to another. Here bonds of fellowship were made that transplanted the southern spirit of prayer to the urban north.

> By 1920, there were twenty Holiness churches in Chicago, all meeting in storefronts or houses. . . . The preacher, or presiding elder, was commonly an uneducated migrant from the South, who had founded the church while working at another job. . . . Members of these congregations

[2] *Ibid.,* p. 50.
[3] *Ibid.,* p. 73.
[4] *Ibid.,* p. 74.
[5] *Ibid.*

spent most of their free time in religious activities: some churches held nightly services, and all of them, in addition to Sunday worship, conducted two or three mid-week prayer meetings and periodic revivals and healing campaigns.[6]

One of the most successful of the early Pentecostal leaders in the city of Chicago was a woman named Elder Lucy Smith. Her All Nations Pentecostal Church was a landmark in the 1930s. This woman was born in Georgia, in the year 1875. She grew up with a deep love for traditional religion, colored by congregational involvement. When she came to Chicago, she joined the Olivet Baptist Church, the leading Baptist church of the city. Still her spirit longed for the "down-home, traditional religion," spontaneous and full of fire.

> In 1916, she organized a one-room prayer meeting in her house; ten years later, after numerous moves and changes, she started to erect her own church building. Lucy Smith, according to one observer, was "a simple, ignorant, untrained woman with deep human sympathies, who believed absolutely in her own power to help and heal other people. Calm and serene in that faith, she has drawn together a following from the back streets of Chicago."[7]

Many of these prayer-meeting-launched storefront churches were Baptist; others were Spiritual; and still others followed various Pentecostal doctrines. Because the normal religious experiences of these groups were attractive to newcomers, the melting pot of the prayer meeting bridged the religious fires of the South into the storefront exuberance of the North.

The growth patterns of the established churches in Chicago depended largely on congregational participation. If the church was highly liturgical with the clergy in leadership, the membership rolls in those early days did not swell like the churches with free congregational participation.

> Many of the new Baptist congregations were ephemeral little storefronts, but others, although beginning in stores or private homes, grew into large and substantial congregations. Pilgrim, Progressive, Provident, Liberty, and Monumental Baptist Churches, all founded between 1916 and 1919, began as prayer meetings in the homes of migrants

---

[6] Allan Spear, *Black Chicago* (Chicago: The University of Chicago Press, 1967), p. 175.
[7] *Ibid.,* p. 176.

recently arrived from the South. Within a decade, all of these congregations had acquired their own buildings and boasted memberships of over five hundred. Primarily migrant churches, they provided a middle ground between the formal, old-time northern congregations and the emotional, uninhibited storefronts.[8]

In summary, we can see how the fervor of prayer from the deep South served to give cohesion to a people who migrated to the North in search of jobs and a better life. The prayers did not change. Indeed, the songs did not. And wherever Black people would bend their knees in prayer, whether in a big church or a small storefront, they would have the same expectation from God and the same desires of their brothers and sisters. Their prayer meeting was their vehicle to community, affirming their personhood and keeping alive their hope for a better day.

Training Ground for Church Leaders

The prayer meeting has served as a kind of field seminary, providing training in Bible studies, speech before people, and the dynamics of leadership in worship. While the major training thrust of this sort occurs in the local church, one could not possibly overlook the place of the home and the community in providing special growth through the experience of prayer and its leadership.

The Home

The home must be credited with doing its part in the development of this prayer tradition. The influence of prayer did not escape the log cabin or the later northern flat. Almost every Black child has had the parental influence of saying a prayer before retiring to bed at night, and for many Black children, a prayer at the beginning of each day. Maya Angelou tells how her grandmother prayed every morning to begin the day.

> During the picking season my grandmother would get out of bed at four o'clock (she never used an alarm clock) and creak down to her knees and chant in a sleep-filled voice, "Our Father, thank you for letting me see this New Day. Thank you that you didn't allow the bed I lay on last night to be my cooling board, nor my blanket my winding sheet. Guide my feet this day along the straight and narrow, and help me to put a bridle on my

[8] *Ibid.,* p. 178.

tongue. Bless this house and everybody in it. Thank you, in the name of your Son, Jesus Christ, Amen."[9]

In addition to prayers uttered at the beginning of the day, Black people have traditionally prayed at the noonday and evening hour.

> Muh great-gran—she name Peggy—I membuh she pray ebry day at sunrise, at noon, an' at sunset. She kneel down wen she pray an at duh en she bow low tree times, facing duh sun.[10]

Noonday prayers were often encouraged by ministers, especially during revival services. All members of the church were encouraged to stop what they were doing and pray for the visitation of God's presence at noon. This custom, with roots in Africa, is very much alive in the Black church today.

Some of the older Blacks had a special prayer day. For many this day was Monday, and for others Friday. "Friday wuz duh day she call huh prayuh day."[11] Whatever the day, Black people used this day to get closer to God, and to secure for themselves spiritual power.

Family prayer meetings in the Black tradition were usually held on a given night during the week. Each member of the family would normally say a Bible verse and then offer a brief prayer. These weekly meetings served as a forum to thrash out problems and to develop individual talent. It was a perfect time to give children an experience of praying to gain confidence in self and to share with others.

The writer had the experience of weekly prayers at home. They were an experience of voluntary prayer participation and were never forced. Prayer was as natural to home as daily meals. It drew the family closer and established strong cords of love between parents and children. Obviously, the custom of family prayers, established coercively, could alienate children and cause them to develop negative attitudes toward the experience of prayer.

The Sunday morning family prayer around the breakfast table has served to reinforce the power of Black prayers. This was a time for Bible quotations, individually shared prayers, and a closing prayer by the man of the house.

[9] Maya Angelou, *I Know Why the Caged Bird Sings* (New York: Bantam Books, 1969), p. 5. Used by permission of Random House, Inc.
[10] Georgia Writers' Project, Works Project Administration, *Drums and Shadows!* (Athens: University of Georgia Press, 1940), p. 141.
[11] *Ibid.,* p. 145.

Other times when family prayers surfaced were the festive gatherings of aunts, uncles, or grandparents. In those days before television and the mass use of radios, the act of singing and praying was indeed a form of entertainment, praise, and family unity. What child would not have enjoyed these unrestrained moments of folk tales, songs, praises, and prayers? Such an experience would send everyone along the way rejoicing. The tradition persists because it does not consist of unnatural and cold piety, but of joy.

Community Prayer Bands

Community prayer bands usually developed around the strong personality of some man or woman. Generally this man or woman had felt some call to evangelize and spread the Word of God. This usually entailed some weekly fasting, visiting of the sick, and weekly prayer sessions.

Several pastoral experiences illustrate the nature of prayer bands. One occurred in the Court Street Baptist Church, Lynchburg, Virginia, one of the oldest Black churches in the South, founded in the year 1861. This church had a reputation of a formal and liturgical worship. Notwithstanding, a woman in this church, convinced that God had healed her of cancer, formed a prayer band of five women. This woman, strong of personality and gifted as a poetess, was a force with which to be reckoned. Every Monday was fasting day. No week passed without a visitation to homes for the elderly and the sick and shut-in, and general evangelistic work.

The significance of this woman and her work revealed that the Black prayer tradition is not the monopoly of the trained clergy, or even the elected officers of the Black church; it is an open prayer tradition, to be used by any person desiring to do so. Prayer bands of this sort often reached persons in the Black community who would possibly be overlooked by the organized church. It also provided a meaningful avenue for lay participation in evangelistic and mission work.

In a word, community prayer bands have provided opportunity for those persons who desired to express themselves in some pastoral role to do so with community support and respect. Historically, Black female leadership has been greatly channeled through this avenue of service.

Female Leadership

Black women who lead in some form of prayer ministry across America seem to owe some of their calling to the inherited role of the African priestess. This is especially true where women, using the title of "Mother," minister to persons in the general areas of healing, family advice, and the normal problems of life. Many lives are constantly touched through this adaptable ministry.

Mother Rosa Artimus Horne, a former seamstress, rose to power among her followers in the city of New York as the "Pray for Me Priestess." [12] "She claimed to have raised thousands of people from the dead besides having made hundreds of the blind see." [13]

The Mt. Sinai Holy Church, founded in Philadelphia in 1924, is another example of the strong prayer leadership of a woman. The founder of this church, Bishop Ida Robinson, was born in Florida. She grew up in Georgia. At the age of seventeen she was converted and began a ministry of prayer bands. She left the South and came to Philadelphia, where she founded this church. One of the strong features of worship in Mt. Sinai Holy Church is prayer. "During services it frequently happens that all members get on their knees and pray aloud simultaneously, each person saying his own prayer." [14]

Examples of women founding churches from prayer bands and carrying on community ministries are indeed numerous. Every major city in America would seem to have some Black woman with a prayer ministry of some sort, calling herself under the general heading "Mother."

Mother Mary of Baltimore, Maryland, has a weekly radio program. On this program she boasts of being able to cure all manner of diseases, to solve problems, and to bring peace to troubled minds.

Several years ago the writer was contacted by one such "Mother" in the city of Philadelphia, Pennsylvania. This Mother desired his assistance in leading a tour of the Holy Land. While he was in her home, she began to give a personal "reading" into the writer's life. A

[12] E. Franklin Frazier and Eric C. Lincoln, *The Negro Church in America* (New York: Schocken Books Inc., 1966), p. 60. Reprinted by permission of Schocken Books, Inc. Copyright © 1963 by the University of Liverpool and © 1974 by Schocken Books, Inc.

[13] *Ibid.*, p. 61.

[14] Arthur Huff Fauset, *Black Gods of the Metropolis* (Philadelphia: University of Pennsylvania Press, 1971), p. 21.

"certain very old officer, who would eventually cause trouble," she said, was in his church. Southern folk wisdom had prepared the writer for this episode, and he knew that this was her way of establishing some sense of power. Throughout her home were statues and apparent places for prayer. Only a fairly mature person would easily escape her mystique. Her counterpart in style, mystique, and total personality can be found wherever Black people live in large numbers.

These women cannot be ignored. They continue to have a following among the poor, the socially dispossessed, and among those who feel that more established doors to solutions are closed.

In a more national sense, however, the sense of the Black Mother's role as Priestess came home in the tragic death of Mrs. Martin Luther King, the mother of the late Dr. Martin Luther King, Jr. At her funeral the Reverend Dr. Ralph David Abernathy described her as "Mother of the Civil Rights Movement of the 1960s." This woman, through fortitude and prayer, always gave the orders to "march on," even during the dark nights of the struggle. Her husband, Dr. Martin Luther King, Sr., in his closing remarks stated, "Everything that has been said about Bunch is true!" In a symbolic way, this woman, even in death, amplified the powerful strength of prayer and undaunted faith that has given courage and creative growth to Black people across many generations. And Providence would have her at the organ at Ebenezer Baptist Church, Atlanta, Georgia, playing the greatest of all prayers, the "Lord's Prayer," when fatally wounded.

A Healing Ground for Physical, Mental, and Spiritual Diseases

In a very exceptional way Black people have been able to sustain the pressures of a segregated and often oppressed life and yet find a way to celebrate the gift of life. This has been a traditional personality trait of Black people and is due to the Black person's way of finding healing and peace through the power of prayer. Recently, however, this healing has shown signs of failure, due mainly to the social rise of Black people and falling away from the Black church. Jack Slater had this in mind in an article he wrote entitled "The Alarming Rise of Suicide Among Black Women." The article was poised against the background of a people who generally have known few suicides, especially among their women. Why, now, should this morbid trend toward suicide claim so many educated and socially arrived persons? The reason given by Jack Slater was a quote from James P. Comer, noted Black psychiatrist at Yale University Medical School. He stated:

> . . . black female suicide may be rising because institutions on which women have traditionally depended are eroding. "The caring, protective systems which black people once found in the church and in the extended family are now not so available to us."[15]

In the traditional Black church every woman could find meaning and sustaining values to cope with the many vicissitudes of life.

In the open prayer meeting everyone could pray, no matter how feeble the effort. Everyone had a personal testimony. "The Lord has healed me" was a proclamation of great worth. "The God of the universe has honored my life to lay his healing hand upon me!"

This letter from G. L. Washington is a testimony to such healing.

> On Sunday morning, August 26, I was taken ill; the doctor was at my beside from 5:00 A.M.–10:30 A.M. and 4:40 P.M. . . . . After I had been in the hospital two weeks, the doctors, running tests and taking X rays, told me they would have to operate. The diagnosis: a tumor of the kidney. They explained that 98% of such cases are malignant, and if that was true in my case, they would remove the kidney. My church held a "Special Prayer Service" for me. Then members came out in large numbers, some got off from work, some postponed or cancelled engagements they had. Something happened.
>
> The doctors decided to take another X ray. According to this picture both kidneys were all right. However, the picture did show a stone in the ureter which was removed by surgery.[16]

For Black people, healing is definitely achieved through prayer. This healing takes place in the name of Jesus. The acts of kneeling, laying on of hands, and coming to the altar may not always take away the cancer or misery, but healing nonetheless has taken place! Prayer itself is healing! A strong magnetism of optimism is generated when the sisters and brothers meet together to call upon the name of the Lord. Here the aches and pains of this mortal body melt away as the Lord God takes over.

Black people do not seem to draw any firm line between mind and

[15] Jack Slater, *Ebony* magazine, vol. 28, no. 11 (September, 1973), p. 158.
[16] Letter from G. L. Washington, minister of the Tabernacle Baptist Church, Washington, D.C., October, 1973.

spirit, soul and body. They believe that healing reaches the total person. They carry with them the belief that the minister, "God's man," can "get a prayer through" where others will fail.

A man and wife came into the writer's office believing in his "special powers." The woman had been under surgery and was still suffering pain. However, they both came, dressed in their best attire, believing that "God's man" could do what their own sincere prayers had failed to do. In addition to praying for their own physical ailments, they wanted prayer that their lives would be totally purged of past and distant sins which they confessed. The woman had known a brief period of infidelity with another man. Now she was convinced her suffering and mental anguish were due to unconfessed sins of the past. Her husband was prepared to accept her sincerity and desired to find complete healing for her body and soul. The writer joined hands with the couple and offered prayer, and the result has been a healthier marriage for the man and his wife.

This psychic need in the corporate minds and spirits of Black people is often exploited and commercially used. The Black person enters prayer with a deeply rooted notion that God's man has contact with power. With such faith, the possibility for healing is present, with or without desired physical results.

Warming Up for Worship

> Reverend, I can remember when I was a boy. Rev. Roane was our pastor. When we got through with Sunday school, the deacons would gather and open up church. When the preacher got up to preach his sermon—well everything was just as hot as fire! [17]

These words were spoken by a deacon. He expressed the common view that prayer meeting ought to warm things up for worship. The order for this warming-up service was always informal. Deacons would assemble at the front of the sanctuary with the deaconesses and missionary sisters sitting somewhere close to the front. The hymns were normally "lined out" in a chanted way and then sung in long-metered style. No pianos or organs were used. The main desire was to get the church "tuned up" for worship. Prayers were interjected between hymns, building in intensity as the service moved along.

[17] Statement by Deacon Moore, personal interview, March, 1974, Baltimore, Maryland.

Charles S. Johnson gave this account of a traditional southern Black church preparing for the main worship.

> After the opening hymn, the congregation is seated; a hard-faced, wiry, dark man remains standing. He is Deacon Eppse, and he prays thus:
> "Blessed Jesus, we thank you for life, the greatest blessing in the world, life. We thank you for the blood that circulates through our bodies. We thank you for the blood and the air so we can stand on our feet. We thank you for the loving hand of mercy bestowed upon us; that Thou are in our midst. Prepare us for our souls' journey through this unfriendly world, and when our life on this earth is ended receive us into Thy home which art in Heaven."
> The congregation sings, "We'll Understand It Better By and By." An elderly brown man of about 65 reads the scripture. There are groans and solemn exclamations from the four men in front of the altar, "Lord have mercy." "Amen." [18]

The reader guided the "devotional service" as a preparation for true worship. Many times deacons would do this kind of sermonizing to create the atmosphere for the preacher who would shortly come.

> We have to slip and straighten up the wick in the candle and lamp. We have to straighten up a car. Just like we have to straighten up a wick so the light will burn, and the car so it will run, we have to straighten up our lives so we can go the way our Lord wants us to go. [19]

Remnants of this pattern of worship still survive in many Black churches. That time between the close of Sunday church school and the beginning of worship, 10:30 to 11:00 A.M., is generally used for this purpose. Still other churches have adopted the practice of assembling with deacons, deaconesses, trustees, and choirs to have a period of song and prayer before going into the main auditorium.

Whatever the method or innovation, the desired result is the sense of high expectancy. The prayer hour generates this expectancy. The historic sense of warming up for worship by prayerfully climbing "Jacob's Ladder" is still being practiced and would appear to be profoundly meaningful in making creative the hour of worship.

The Old-Fashioned Mourners' Bench

No experience in this prayer tradition was expected to bring more

---

[18] Charles Johnson, *Growing Up in the Black Belt* (Washington, D.C.: American Council on Education, 1941), p. 137.
[19] *Ibid.*, pp. 137-138.

from God than the "mourners'" bench. This was usually the front pew in the church. Here the mourners sat directly in front of the pulpit. In some places, mourners were expected to sit with their heads bowed, supposedly in prayer, awaiting the moment of conversion. In other places, this act was not required.

On one Sunday the preacher had finished his homily. He had painted the glorious vision of heaven and denounced the woes of hell. He had proclaimed that "the Lord is here, right now, waiting to save whosoever will"! On the front row sat an old man and four children. They were on the "anxious seat." The door of the church of Christ was now opened. Shouts of "Amen" and "Thank God" filled the air. The church was filled with the spirit. All eyes were turned on the sinners. Suddenly the minister came down from the pulpit and stood in front of the seekers. He stretched forth his hand crying, "Come to Jesus!" No one moved. Without a word, a sister and a deacon came over and began talking with the mourners. Now the deacon knelt down, his hand on top of the sinner's head, possibly a relative or someone he had invited to church, and he began to pray. He was followed by the sister. Spiritual momentum was built higher and higher. Quickly the children leaped up rejoicing! Now the church concentrated on the old man. After much tarrying in prayer, the old man jumped up shouting, "Thank God, I been redeemed!"

Such an experience might happen in any church, especially those churches strongly influenced by the ways of the South. Some typical lines from a prayer that might be offered at the altar came from a Reverend Pride, who pastored the Oak Grove Baptist Church, in a rural district of Virginia.

> We are not able to save a soul, but the power is in thy hand. Master, this evening we have three sitting here. They are saying by ways and actions that they want Thee in their lives. Oh, Oh Law'dy, Oh Law'dy, you can save in the twinkling of an eye. Oh, Jesus, we want you to come this way right now. Oh, Jesus, we are coming right now on pleading terms of mercy. Oh, Lord, please, please, Jesus, please reach down right now, Master. Change us, change us all around. Oh, Lord, Lord, we know that salvation is free.[20]

This spontaneous prayer drove home the import of the moment. The desires of the entire congregation were verbalized in language

[20] Observation from prayer, Oak Grove Baptist Church, Massies Mill, Virginia, 1962.

that made a strong plea to God. The one big aim was for prayer to pull the sinner through.

While Reverend Pride was praying, some persons were moaning. Others were rubbing their hands. Some were shouting. Still others were looking heavenward, as if speaking with God. All these actions and expressions merged together, generating the sense of the one basic need, the moving power of the Holy Spirit. After the prayer, a song caught up the feeling:

> Oh, where you running, sinner?
> Oh, you can't hide.
> Oh, where you running, sinner?
> Oh, you can't hide.
> Oh, where you running, sinner?
> Oh, you can't hide.
> You can't hide, sinner; you can't hide.[21]

The following statements are reactions various persons have had to this experience. One thirteen-year-old girl in Bolivar County, Mississippi, said:

> I sat up there and something say, "Now come to me, come to me now," so I just got up and went on down to the preacher and testified. It didn't strike me bad like it do some folks, but I went anyhow.[22]

A seventeen-year-old fourth-grade farm youth in Madison County, Alabama, told how he had a vision:

> I seen or dreamed something. I thought I saw some dogs, some lean hounds, and I thought that meant that old Satan was running me. So I knew I'd better get religion, and I been a lot different since.[23]

A deacon tells his account of being on the mourners' bench:

> When I was at the mourner's bench praying to God asking him to save my soul, the spirit of the devil came to me and told me to curse God. My tongue cleaved to the roof of my mouth. This made me get stronger in Christ. This is why I know I've got religion.[24]

So deep is the mourners' bench "mystique" in the hearts and minds of Black people, that even today a kind of open division exists in the

---

[21] Traditional Black folk spiritual.
[22] Johnson, op. cit., p. 160.
[23] Ibid.
[24] Deacon Moses Williams, personal interview, Baltimore, Maryland, March, 1974.

Black church between those persons who "got something" and those who can testify to no pointed change. When new members are being taken into the church, those who simply "shake the preacher's hand" are not looked upon with as much joyful satisfaction as those who come readily, with tear-stained eyes and some word of testimony. There is a deep conviction that the believer must undergo some genuine, emotionally transforming experience. This belief is expressed in the oft-repeated words:

> I looked at my hands
> and they looked new
> I looked at my feet
> and they did, too![25]

The key to the bench and to salvation is prayer. Here the Black man dared to see what God would do. When the sinner got up from the bench, it was proof beyond doubt that God was in his church, working mightily among his people.

Altar Call and Blessing Line

In many churches the same mighty workings of God seen at the mourners' bench were expected in the altar call and the blessing line. This expectation was strengthened by the belief that "God's man" had special contact with unseen power. The African tradition, the long night of slavery, and continued oppression helped to build a style calling for quick and specific blessing. Those persons who seized upon this need, claiming themselves to be conjurers, healers, root doctors, and the like helped to fan the fires of expectancy. The need of a people to find practical remedies for ailments, without access to doctor's medicine and developed medical treatment, gave a free hand to the conjurers and the prophets during the long night of servitude, and since. Today, among many Black people, the power of faith and prayer is applied and tried in any act where some quick blessing is needed.

The writer's experience on the island of Haiti, studying and learning the ways of the people, confirmed the high sense of spiritual communion and of anticipation among some Black people of prayer. It was astonishing to observe the degree to which Haitians, involved

---

[25] Traditional Black folk statement uttered in prayers, testimonies, and sermons.

in a voodoo service, could move in and out of the spirit as they sought contact with various gods. It was easily observed how this prayerful spirit relationship colored all of life, creating blessings for the obedient and providing for the disobedient some curse.

Common African ancestry has provided the innate impetus of prophets, priests, medicine men, conjurers, mothers, and mystics, who peddle their wares especially among Black people. The one who can best generate the believer's faith in his or her power to cure is generally the one who succeeds.

The altar prayer appeals to those who feel the need to act on their faith. Here the typical storefront church surely excels. The sense of family togetherness, freedom from cold tradition, and readiness to adapt to the need of any moment create an openness for what the Lord can do.

> During the 1920s when southern Negroes were flocking to Harlem in New York City, it was found that only 54 out of 140 churches in Harlem were housed in regular church structures. The remainder were of the "storefront" type which had been organized by preachers, many of whom were exploiters and charlatans. They based their appeal on the Negro's desire to find salvation in the next world and to escape from sickness and the insecurities of this world. One of these churches advertised:
> We Believe that all Manner of Disease Can Be Cured
> Jesus is the Doctor
> Services on Sunday [26]

Bargaining with the God of Game and Gain

No comprehensive study of this subject could overlook examples of prayerful bargaining with God. Here the believer comes before God with some "offering," expecting to receive a blessing in return. The blessing can be a "number" expected surely to "hit" or win, in the daily lottery. It could be a blessed handkerchief, guaranteed to remove all misery and pain, because the fee for prayer was paid. At times it is an anointment with oil, or the gift of an emblem or trinket, all supposed to bring good fortune from God. Excerpts from the following letter illustrate the kind of self-appointed prophet who comes into the Black community seeking monetary gain from the mystique of prayer.

[26] Frazier, *op. cit.*, p. 54.

My dear Christian Friend:

Just a few lines to let you know that I will be in the City of Baltimore, Maryland. . . .

Everybody knows what I am and what I can do, because every time I come to town I break the bank and number bankers all over the country is mad at me because they know what I can do. . . .

I have also with me the world's biggest High John The Conqueror Root and all you need to do is touch it one time for good luck. . . .

Until I see you, keep looking up and remember that the Lord will provide for those who trust in Him.

The World's Most Amazing Prophet,
Bishop Clyde Jefferson[27]

This letter is typical of the appeal of this type of "prophet" and "miracle man," who plays on the mystique of roots, handkerchiefs, even the Bible, always assuring the hopeful that a blessing awaits them—for a fee, of course.

Clarence Cobbs, founder and pastor of the First Church of Deliverance, Chicago, Illinois, and president of the Metropolitan Spiritual Churches in America, presided over a service in Baltimore. Before the close of the service, he gave the believers opportunity to come down front for prayer. Here a candle was given each believer who told "Preacher," as he is affectionately called, what he or she desired from God. A monetary offering was left as the candle was given. The candle was to be taken home, placed on one's altar and used as a continuous source of God's blessings.

Some months later the writer was in Chicago and throughout the day was taxied about Chicago by a member of "Preacher's" church. He asked, "Do people get results from setting up candles provided by the church in their homes?" The brother, who freely talked as the day went on, said, "Yes! One just does not realize what the candles mean to poor people, forgotten and kicked about! These candles bring much joy into their lives." He was asked, "Do you know whether people are healed through these candles?" He said that his own life was a wreck and "this personal altar in his home had kept before him a sacred strength, providing worship day by day."[28]

One can surmise that where some faith object, such as a candle, is

[27] Letter, February, 1974, under heading as stated above, "The World's Most Amazing Prophet, Bishop Clyde Jefferson."

[28] Personal interview with Joseph Jackson, Chicago, Illinois, April, 1974.

present, all good fortunes will be ascribed to its charm or power. This is true of dreams also.

Walker Stewart was a deacon from a Black church in Bradenton, Florida. He was convinced he had risen from poverty in the deep South through a "dream." In this dream God showed him a certain number to play in the lottery. He played and won. Later, as a man of considerable means, he was literally convinced God had blessed him through a "hit."

This same belief was expressed in the Baltimore *Afro-American,* dated October 13, 1973. The headline read as follows:

$1 MILLION WON IN LOTTERY BY PRAYING WAITRESS

The column reads:

> Mrs. Doris L. Hill, 46, LaPlata, Md., the stately, quiet mother of three who won the second Million Dollar prize in Maryland State Lottery history, had a feeling something good was coming to her.
>
> The night before the Wednesday drawing at the Baltimore Lord Baltimore Hotel, she prayed, "Help me win. So few of my people have gotten anything."
>
> According to her daughter, Miss Muriel Gray, 29, a beauteous United Airlines' stewardess, "My mother was calm and sincere. . . . She read her Bible the night before and she prayed." [29]

She is certainly little different from Joe Louis, who knocked out his opponents in the ring and then thanked his mother and God. The recent boxing champion, George Foreman, won his heavyweight crown from Joe Frazier in Kingston, Jamaica, and immediately reacted by clearing his dressing room, where he fell on his knees in prayer. "I thanked God for everything, for everybody, and for the determination he gave me to see it through." [30] It is clear that the masses of Black people do not separate blessings into sacred and secular ones. Any blessing that lifts the burden of life is seen as coming from God. It is therefore not inappropriate, in a part of the prayer tradition, to ask God for anything, or to bargain in prayer.

Praying the Old Year Out—The New Year In

The prayer meeting that gathered for the purpose of praying the

[29] Baltimore *Afro-American,* October 13, 1973.
[30] John Reddy, "Making of a Champion," *Reader's Digest,* vol. 105, no. 629 (September, 1974), p. 45.

old year out and the new year in was traditionally called the watch-night service. In many Black churches, this was the most important prayer meeting of the Christian year. Here the saints gathered to thank God for keeping them through the past year and to be found in a state of prayer, on bended knees in God's house, when the clock struck twelve and the new year began.

The act of being on bended knee at the midnight hour was supported by the spiritual belief among Black people that a good ending and beginning were necessary ingredients for the Christian's year. Black people believed God would forgive the sins of the past year in a special way on this night that closed the year and opened up the new year. This golden moment afforded the godly person the annual opportunity to make a new resolve to live a holier life.

This was also a night for the saints to give their "testimonies" and make their "determinations." [31] The writer remembers with freshness those "testimonies" and "determinations" the saints made in the rural Baptist churches of Alabama. "Children, I have been coming up the rough side of the mountain all year. Along the way I thought I wouldn't make it. But I kept on praying, and the Lord has brought me through, and I am here to tell the story." [32] This typical testimony was followed by a typical "determination." "Church, I haven't been as good this year as I ought, I know I have fallen short of the mark, but I want y'all to pray for me, that I might overcome my faults and failures." [33] "Amen! Amen! help him, Lawd," responded the church.

Generally it was the minister, "God's man," who was praying for the flock during the all-important twelve o'clock midnight hour. Only he could unite God's people with divine power at a depth suitable for this occasion.

The long tradition of this meeting was recounted by the ex-slave who told this account of his grandmother from Africa.

"She tell me bout duh hahves time wen duh folks stay up all night an shout. At sun-up dey all sing an pray and say dey live bettuh and be mo tankful duh nex year."

[31] A testimony was a personal statement of what God had done in the believer's life. A determination was a statement the believer made, committing himself or herself to live a better life or to overcome some personal fault.

[32] Traditional Black testimony heard in Black churches.

[33] Traditional Black "determination," heard in Black churches.

"Was your 'gran' grown up when she came from Africa?"
"No'm, she wuz jis a leedle ting."[34]

The writer has attended this annual prayer meeting since he was a boy in Alabama. The psychological sense of security that comes from being on bended knee at this midnight hour is really influential. Even today, many Black persons will rush into church a few minutes before the midnight hour to be sure they are on their knees to welcome in the New Year.

When this prayer service was all over and the New Year had begun, saints got up from their knees, shouting, singing, praying, and praising God, wishing everyone present a "Happy New Year."

The Altar Call—Institutionalized Church

In the previous discussion of the altar and blessing line, much of it involved people outside the "organized church" and certainly not in the strong, established churches. Notwithstanding, the established churches have their altar calls and seek essentially the same results.

Members of the Tabernacle Baptist Church, Selma, Alabama, often rushed forward, following D. V. Jemison's Sunday sermons, to shake his hand. There was a feeling in the church that a blessing could be gained from shaking God's servant's hand. This was a leading church in the city with an image of intellect and social prestige. Yet the people had a need for sharing in the divine moment of going to the altar.

William H. Dinkins, past-president of Selma University, Selma, Alabama, was a member of this church and a graduate of Brown University. Many times this man, speaking at Selma University as president, has urged students and faculty to shake the preacher's hand by coming to the altar, as an extension of the message and a linkage to God's divine favor. The practice of doing this is current in this school until this very day. It is even more common to find persons coming forward for prayer after the sermon and the invitation.

The spirit and wording of the altar prayer generally followed the impact of the worship, especially the sermon. Sometimes this prayer was before the sermon. In any case, it reached the needs of those persons who came to the altar as well as those who remained in their

[34] Georgia Writers' Project, *op. cit.,* p. 145.

pews. The prayer called forth the deep reservoir of strength latent in every person.

Altar prayers are employed in a meeting as august as that for ministerial leaders and executives of the American Baptist Churches and Progressive National Baptist Convention, who gathered in Chicago, Illinois, for the "Fund of Renewal," proposing to raise seven and one-half million dollars for minority causes. After the sermon, an altar prayer was called. Around the altar gathered many ministers, holding hands together. Thomas Kilgore, minister of Second Baptist Church, Los Angeles, California, and past-president of the American Baptist Churches, offered the prayer:

> Eternal God our Father, we thank Thee for this experience together. We have come here in the interest of the Fund of Renewal. We thank Thee that in the hearts of members of the American Baptist and the Progressive National Baptist Conventions, this movement started. We thank Thee that we have been able to stay together, to pray together and to move forward, even over pitfalls, and to come thus far.
>
> We are grateful for the encounter that we have had here today, as we have spoken out of our hearts. We thank Thee for all the messages of hope that have come to us today from everyone that has spoken. We thank Thee for this message of hope and inspiration tonight, and may each one of us leave here this evening, our Father, with a greater determination to preach and live Jesus every day of our lives. Let us look upon the future of this movement with hope, putting behind it all that we can, giving ourselves fully to Thee.
>
> And now, O Lord, give us a good night's rest and bring us back together in the morning in peace and love, as we deal with the day ahead.
>
> Thank you, Lord, for everything. Thank you that we can be numbered as your children. Thank you that your grace has saved us, and that we can be here involved in the work of your church.
>
> And now may the grace of God, the fellowship of Jesus Christ, and the communion of the Holy Spirit, be with you this night and forevermore. Amen.[35]

Here the prayer caught the thrust and goal of the meeting and verbalized it in such a way that everyone left with one mind. Effectively executed, the altar prayer can always be the creative moment of worship where all that has gone before is lifted up, synthesized, and given as a challenge to God's people in renewal and hope.

[35] Prayer of Thomas Kilgore, Chicago, Illinois, March, 1974.

There are other major functions that this creative prayer tradition serves. The whole scope includes purification, inner release, and concrete action to express faith and to move depressed souls out of the stupor of spiritual and physical paralysis. The altar prayer tradition is also a way of "making it" through life. Attention is turned to these matters in the following chapter.

5

Other Functions of the Black Prayer Tradition

The human need to have some way to express the deepest desires of the soul is normal in the best of situations. It becomes acute when social pressures are multiplied through oppressive forces of segregation and discrimination and all the accompanying methods used to hold Black people down. The fact that Black people have not turned en masse to suicides as a way out of life is due in part to the inner release of prayer. Prayer has been a way of emptying one's life of frustrations, anger, bitterness, and sorrow.

Purification and Inner Release

Catholic persons traditionally go to a priest for confession and counsel. Rich persons consult a psychiatrist. Black people take their "burdens to the Lord." Their sense of the real presence of God means that they can really tell God what is troubling them. They take their burdens to the Lord and leave them there!

The pastoral prayer in the average Black church is filled with statements designed, in large measure, to bring inner release. A few examples follow:

> Lord, we know we are living in a mean world, but you promised to be with us and see us through.

> Somebody here is in trouble! Somebody didn't sleep all night long! Somebody is on his way to surgery! Somebody can't make ends meet! But, Lord, we know all power is in Thy Hand.

> Our Father, we know thou art a heart fixer and a mind regulator. We know thou art a problem solver and a burden bearer. Have mercy right now![1]

All these statements, so familiar to this tradition, are designed to provoke inner release.

Black people tend to believe that prayer has not been effective when one's burdens are not lifted. In simple language, prayer must make the believer "feel better"! When this does not happen, it is felt that the prayer did not "get through." One of the main reasons prayer does not "get through" is insincerity in the heart.

Dr. Martin Luther King, Jr., knew the Black person's traditional sense of sincerity undergirding prayer when he began publicly to preach the difficult doctrine of "Love Thine Enemy" in Montgomery, Alabama. In 1955 when King's home was bombed and Black people were ready to react with violence, King checked this potential mob reaction by saying to those present in front of his home, "Put up your guns; throw away your bricks and bottles; put away your knives. We cannot allow ourselves to fall so low as to adopt the methods of our oppressors. Let us go home and pray for those who hate us, knowing that God will see us through."[2]

Here was an example of inner release of potentially violent passions and yet the encouragement of the positive and powerful force of prayer. Indeed, throughout the Montgomery bus boycott, Black prayers were used for inner release of potentially violent reactions, while sustaining some sense of direction toward freedom and the beloved community for all men.

[1] Traditional Black prayer lines.
[2] Dr. Martin Luther King, Jr., preacher and civil rights leader, heard by the writer, Montgomery, Alabama, 1955.

Prayer as Song and Inner Release

There has always existed a close relationship between song and prayer. The musical chant of the traditional Black prayer has always been interchangeable with lines from music. John Lovell, Jr., has given us this insight:

> Prayer is another literary form in which the spiritual specializes. "It's Me, O Lord," is one of the best prayers because it places responsibility directly on the singer, nobody else. If he is standing in the need of prayer, he is ready to shoulder his responsibility.
>
> Other striking prayers, which qualify as literature, are "Ev'ry Time I Feel de Spirit," "Keep Me f'om Sinkin' Down," "Oh, My Good Lord, Show Me de Way," and "Come Here Lord!" In this last one, the singer commands the Lord in the name of sinners. One of the stanzas of "Come Here Lord!" carries a touching warning,
>> Some seek God's face, but don't seek right,
>> Pray a little by day and none by night.[3]

Howard Thurman declares that "the most universally beloved of all the hymns about Jesus is the well known, 'Were you there when they crucified my Lord?'"[4] Here the Black person works out an identification with the cross that is universal in its deepest meaning. "The inference is that the singer was *there*: 'I know what he went through because I have met him in the high places of pain, and I claim him as my brother.'"[5]

Thus is seen the close connection between prayer and song. Both are deep expressions of the Black person's understanding of God in the light of the problems of evil and suffering. The traditional prayer meeting has always wedded these fundamental expressions of the soul. Even today a soft musical background is normally provided while prayer is uttered in the Black church. What matters is reaching persons at a deep level to lift feelings and lighten burdens.

A Way of Making It Through Life

What does one do when he is stricken with polio at the tender age of two, and his limbs never develop? This question was provoked by the

---

[3] John Lovell, Jr., *Black Song: The Forge and the Flame* (New York: The Macmillan Company, 1972), pp. 376-377.
[4] Howard Thurman, *Deep River* (New York: Harper & Row, Publishers, 1955), p. 22.
[5] *Ibid.,* p. 23.

following story of a young man. Polio had rendered his body powerless to function as other young men. He did have a love for painting. His love for painting, supported by the spiritual strength of his grandmother, led him to prayer. The following are his own words:

> I remember I was fifteen years old, I was painting on this portrait and having trouble getting the likeness of it. I went downstairs and asked my mother and grandma what should I do. They agreed that the portrait just didn't look right; so my grandma said, "Why don't you ask God?"
>
> I went back upstairs and got on my knees. I can't remember exactly what I said, but I fell asleep and when I woke up, it was dark with a light shining through the window on the picture. I got scared and turned on the lights and looked out the window, but the light wasn't there.
>
> So I started working on the painting again, on the eyes where the light had been. When I showed it to my mother and grandma again, they agreed it looked just like the man. After that I sort of felt God was guiding my hand. After finishing each picture, I thank God for helping me.[6]

Now an accomplished artist, having achieved a level of competence and proficiency which many better-known colleagues might envy, Thomas Stockett typifies the Black philosophy of "making it anyhow!" It crops up in all walks of life, always asserting the dogged tenacity popularized by the late Congressman Adam Clayton Powell of New York City, when he cried out, "Keep the faith, Baby."

"Keep the faith" means having a prayer always in one's heart. It is a constant word, "Pray for me." It is an endless statement to the pastor, "Reverend, I just can't make it without prayer."

Among Black people, even those in the medical field rely upon prayer. Gene Bartlett tells the story of going to the bedside of a patient who had not spoken for days. A Black nurse happened to be in the room. He was about to wait for her to excuse herself when she stated, "I'll join you in prayer." As he prayed, Bartlett states, the nurse responded, "Please, Lord, oh, please, Lord!" When the prayer was concluded, the sick patient flashed her eyes and spoke for the first time in days. The fact that the nurse felt totally at ease with prayer is suggestive of a prayer conditioning she had previously known. Prayer for her was natural and totally expected in the day-by-day affairs of life.

Dr. I. Bradshaw Higgins is chief of surgeons at Provident Hospital, Baltimore, Maryland. Once Dr. Higgins came in to see the patient on

[6] The *News American,* Baltimore, October 6, 1973, p. 19.

whom he was scheduled to operate the following morning. Higgins prayerfully talked with the patient and told her that he was just an instrument in God's hand. "My job was to operate," Higgins said, "and I, too, was looking to God to provide healing as only God could do." When asked, "Do you always have this kind of prayerful meeting with your patients before an operation?" Higgins responded:

> You see, I am from Kingston, Jamaica. My father was a superintendent and prayed all the time. He has left in me the power of prayer. Why, I could not live without prayer.[7]

This Black physician has not only done his job well, but also he was recently honored by the citizens of Baltimore for being one of the moving spirits in the building of an all new Provident Hospital for the community of Baltimore, Maryland. He has openly given credit to the power of God, expressed through prayer, for his accomplishments in life.

The experience of visiting patients in the hospital, about to undergo surgery or suffering general pain, helps to reinforce this thought. By and large, these patients will tell you quickly, "Reverend, I'm trusting in the Lord." And then when pains are extremely heavy, one hears the groans, "Lord, have mercy."

Ninety-five percent of radio mail received through the writer's church radio and prayer ministries seeks some aid through prayer.

October 1, 1973

Dear Dr. Carter,
    Just a note to let you know how much dial-a-prayer has helped me through a very trying time in my life. . . .

October 21, 1973

Mr. Carter,
    I have listened to your program on Sunday morning and Sunday evening, and I really enjoy it. I do believe that you are God's messenger. You have really given me confidence in my prayers. My problem is that three children and myself go to church without my wife. The children and myself are praying and hoping that some day she will go. We love to have her with us. So please pray for us. Thank you.[8]

---

[7] Interview with Dr. I. Bradshaw Higgins, by the writer, Baltimore, February 17, 1972.

[8] Letters on file in the New Shiloh Baptist Church, Baltimore, 1973.

It has been said that the American Black person lives life from one crisis to another. Without doubt, Black prayer language reflects this. Even when circumstances are calm and placid, a Black person's theology will reflect an image of just "making it through life." In prayers he or she is forever "climbing a high mountain" or "going through a deep valley." These symbols of rugged human struggle are needed in the mind-view of a people whose history has taken them from oppression to the present struggle for liberation. However well off a Black person may be, financially or intellectually, he or she shares vicariously the language and spirit of the brother or sister who may not have made it as well. Even good fortune has rigid limits. The Black person is aware that we all must "keep the faith" or perish and chooses to "keep the faith," while using the thrust of prayer as a creative weapon of social change.

6

The Black Prayer Tradition as a Weapon of Social Change

No study of the civil rights movement of Black people, from slavery until today, could be complete without acknowledging the undergirding force of prayer. This prayer tradition has historically motivated and given cohesion to the liberation drive of Black people. It has been used by Black women to instill hope in the lives of their children and provide ways to freedom for youth and adult alike. It has undergirded national movements, such as the National Association for the Advancement of Colored People, the Southern Christian Leadership Conference, the Opportunities Industrialization Centers, and the efforts of ministers in local communities, to call attention to social injustices. This prayer tradition remains as a spiritual platform on which broad elements of the Black community can gather to express common concerns to the broader community.

Liberation Through Prayer

When Israel was in Egypt's land, slaves under Pharaoh, they turned to the one power available, prayer. When the Black people were in bondage in the new world, they, too, turned to prayer. The hard forces of a cruel and inhuman existence forced on them the necessity to pray. They quickly made the transition from ancestral African religions to the almighty name of Jesus. The available images of life exalted the White man and oppressed the Black man. In a world like this the Black community found hope in prayer. The Black men and women used this spiritual force to carve avenues of liberation for themselves and their fellow citizens.

Henry "Box" Brown, a slave from Richmond, Virginia, told how his mother instilled in him the power of prayer, eventually leading to his liberation.

> . . . my sister became anxious to have her soul converted, and shaved the hair from her head, as many of the slaves thought they could not be converted without doing this. My mother reproved her, and began to tell her of God who dwelt in heaven, and that she must pray to him to convert her.[1]

Henry "Box" Brown never forgot what his mother said. It stirred in him the belief that God could direct his escape from bondage if he would ask him in sincerity.

> At length, after praying earnestly to Him, who seeth afar off, for assistance, in my difficulty, suddenly, as if from above, there darted into my mind these words, "Go and get a box, and put yourself into it." I pondered the words over in my mind. "Get a box?" thought I; "what can this mean?" But I was "not disobedient unto the heavenly vision," and I determined to put into practice this direction, as I considered it, from my heavenly Father.[2]

Henry "Box" Brown executed his idea, and arrived in Philadelphia, Pennsylvania, "praising God from whom all blessings flow!" By his own testimony, the seed for freedom was given him by the prayerful instructions of his mother.

Booker T. Washington, famed educator and founder of Tuskegee Institute, credits his desire for freedom to his mother. He wrote:

[1] Charles Stearns, *Narrative of Henry Box Brown* (Boston: Brown & Stearns, 1849), pp. 17-18.
[2] *Ibid.,* p. 59.

"I was awakened one morning, before the break of day, by my mother bending over me, where I lay on a bundle of rags in the corner of my master's kitchen, and hearing her pray that Abraham Lincoln and his soldiers might be successful and that I might some day be free." At that moment the small boy caught his first glimpse of what it might mean to be free.[3]

Booker T. Washington's daughter observed the powerful force of prayer in his life and attributed his major accomplishments to this practice.

We never at home began the day without prayer, and we closed the day with prayer in the evening. He read the Bible to us at breakfast each day and prayed; that was never missed. Really he prayed all the time. His faith built Tuskegee.[4]

Harriet Tubman, a slave of extraordinary powers, was convinced her leadership was given to her through prayers to God. Her freedom, which she eventually won, was not for selfish purposes. This brave woman returned so often to the South, freeing slaves, that a bounty of $40,000 was placed upon her head, dead or alive.

On one occasion she instructed a messenger: "Read my letter to the old folks, and give my love to them, and tell my brothers to be always *watching unto prayer,* and when the *good old ship of Zion comes along, to be ready to step aboard.*"[5]

Thomas Garrett, the Wilmington Quaker, was so impressed with this woman's sense of prayer that he said:

For in truth I never met with any person, of any color, who had more confidence in the voice of God, as spoken direct to her soul. She has frequently told me that she talked with God, and he talked with her every day of her life, and she has declared to me that she felt no more fear of being arrested by her former master, or any other person, than she did in the State of New York, or Canada, for she said she never ventured only where God sent her, and her faith in a Supreme Power truly was great.[6]

In this same liberation movement must be placed the life of Sojourner Truth. She was born a slave in Henley, Ulster County, New York, about 1797. Her lack of formal education could not

[3] Basil Matthews, *Booker T. Washington* (Cambridge: Harvard University Press, 1948), p. 18.
[4] *Ibid.,* p. 190.
[5] Sarah H. Bradford, *Scenes in the Life of Harriet Tubman* (Auburn: W. J. Moses, Printer, 1869), p. 57.
[6] *Ibid.,* p. 49.

destroy her spiritual genius. Her first name was Isabella. She announced one morning to her employer that she was leaving. "The Lord is going to give me a new home, Mrs. Whiting, and I am going away. . . . I cannot stay. I have heard a voice from heaven. It tells me to go. . . . Farewell, friends—I must be about my Father's business."[7]

Walking along a road in Brooklyn, a new name came to Isabella. "Sojourner! There now," she said to herself, "the name has come. Sojourner. That's it. Because I am to travel up and down the land, showing the people their sins, and being a sign unto them."[8] Sojourner continued her travels, crying out, "Oh, God, give me a name with a *handle* to it."

"Sojourner's guiding voice called down to her, as if from God above, 'Sojourner Truth.'"[9]

> The excited woman leaped in the air for joy.
> "Why," she exclaimed, "thank you, God. That is a good name. Thou art my last Master, and thy name is Truth; and Truth shall be my abiding name till I die!"[10]

Everywhere this champion of freedom went, she busied herself with praying and later with proclaiming God's Word, in private homes, camp meetings, and eventually in the White House. This brave woman had the following conversation with Abraham Lincoln:

> "Mr. President," she said, "when you first took your seat, I feared you would be torn to pieces, for I likened you unto Daniel, who was thrown into the lion's den."
> Abraham Lincoln looked down on Sojourner Truth and said, "They have not done it yet."
> . . . Sojourner continued.
> "If the lions did not tear you to pieces, I knew that it would be God that saved you. And I said if he spared me, I would see you before the four years expired. He has done so, and now I am here to see you for myself."
> The President said, "I congratulate you on being spared to come to Washington to make this visit."
> "I thank God that you have been spared," said Sojourner, "for you are the best president who has ever taken the seat."[11]

---

[7] Arthur Huff Fauset, *Sojourner Truth: God's Faithful Pilgrim* (Chapel Hill: The University of North Carolina Press, 1938), pp. 106-107.
[8] *Ibid.*, p. 109.
[9] *Ibid.*, p. 110.
[10] *Ibid.*, p. 111.
[11] *Ibid.*, p. 147.

Nat Turner, the celebrated insurrectionist of Southampton County, Virginia, declared that all of his instructions came from God. He believed God had some special purpose for him. His peers about him thought he was a prophet with divine wisdom. He stated that all his "time, not devoted to my master's service, was spent either in prayer, or in making experiments in casting differing things in molds made of earth, in attempting to make paper, gunpowder, and many other experiments, which, although I could not perfect, yet convinced me of their practicability, if I had the means."[12]

> Knowing the influence I had obtained over the minds of my fellow-servants (not by conjuring and such like tricks, for to them I always spoke of such things with contempt), but by the communion of the Spirit, whose revelations I often communicated to them; and they believed and said my wisdom came from God. I now began to prepare them for my purpose, by telling them something was about to happen that would terminate in fulfilling the great promise that had been made to me.[13]

The rest is now history. Nat Turner with a band of seventy slaves began his insurrection in Southampton County, Virginia, on August 13, 1831, and went on unchecked for three days and three nights. This prayer-generated rebellion sparked embers of freedom in many Black hearts, far and wide.

The very articulate slave liberationist Frederick Douglass also felt the influence of the Black prayer tradition. He has left on record the interesting account of his early experiences in prayer. A certain "Uncle" Isaac Copper told the children to say everything he said.

> "Our Father"—this we repeated after him with promptness and uniformity—"who art in Heaven" was less promptly and uniformly repeated, and the old gentleman paused in the prayer to give us a short lecture, and to use his switches on our backs.[14]

The poignancy of one of his prayers, lifted up to God while overlooking the waters of the Chesapeake Bay, is haunting with its yearning for freedom. In his biography he said:

> I have often, in the deep stillness of a summer's Sabbath, stood all

---

[12] Thomas C. Gray, *The Confessions of Nat Turner, Leader of the Late Insurrection in Southampton, Va.* (Miami: Mnemosyne Publishing Inc., 1969), p. 4.
[13] *Ibid.*
[14] Frederick Douglass, *Life and Times of Frederick Douglass* (New York: The Crowell-Collier Publishing Company, 1962), p. 43.

alone upon the banks of that noble bay, and traced, with saddened heart and tearful eye, the countless number of sails moving off to the mighty ocean. My thoughts would compel utterance, and there, with no audience but the Almighty, I would pour out my soul's complaint in my rude way with an apostrophe to the moving multitude of ships.

"You are loosed from your moorings, and free. I am fast in my chains, and am a slave! . . . O, that I were free! O, that I were on one of your gallant decks, and under your protecting wing! Alas! betwixt me and you the turbid waters roll. Go on, go on; O that I could also go! Could I but swim! If I could fly! O, why was I born a man, of whom to make a brute! The glad ship is gone—she hides in the dim distance. I am left in the hell of unending slavery. O, God, save me! God, deliver me! Let me be free! Is there any God? Why am I a slave? I will run away. I will not stand it. Get caught or get clear, I'll try it. . . . I had as well be killed running as die standing. . . . Try it? Yes! God helping me, I will."[15]

The Black prayer tradition found perfect flow in George Washington Carver, noted scientist.

"Contact thy Creator. Learn how to tune in with Him, and He will—through you—work miracles. He will guide you to peace, happiness, prosperity—to all your heart's desires." These were the words I heard Dr. Carver pour out to students who attended his volunteer extracurricular Bible Class, held once each week during the school year at Tuskegee Institute, founded by Booker T. Washington at Tuskegee, Alabama.[16]

George Washington Carver was affectionately called "professor" around the campus at Tuskegee. Students often jokingly asked him, "Where have you been?"

Bursting into a hearty laugh, he then waved his hand and said, "I have been exhibiting some of the products made from the peanut, and discovered from long contact with our Creator."

"What were these things?" we asked.

Naming but a few, he answered: "Breakfast food, coffee, buttermilk, pepper, cocoa flour, oleomargarine, beverages, medicines and cosmetics. . . . You, too, in your chosen field," he added, "can do as much by tuning in—by contacting Him."

"How?" someone asked. . . .

"The promise is that he who prayeth in secret is rewarded openly," were the words the professor began with. . . . "Pray in silence. Ask Him for guidance. Keep your thoughts pure. Forget yourself. Know that you are an

---

[15] *Ibid.,* p. 125.

[16] Alvin D. Smith, *George Washington Carver, Man of God* (Middletown, Ohio: Perry Printing Co., 1961), Copyright © 1954 by Alvin D. Smith. All rights reserved. Reprinted by permission of Exposition Press, Inc. Hicksville, NY 11801.

instrument through which your Creator wishes to pour out some blessing for others."[17]

This great man has left us a legacy of communing with God, of talking with the birds, flowers, plants, and nature. He has also left us a vast number of items derived from his experiments with the sweet potato and the peanut.

Another testimony to the power of prayer was heard at the dedication of a new building at a school for girls, in Washington, D.C., founded by the late Nannie Helen Burroughs. One of the speakers stated: "Nannie Helen Burroughs stood in a cornfield, before the school existed, and declared by faith and fervent prayer that a school would be erected here to carry on the work of Christ in training Christian women."[18]

In the city of Baltimore, Maryland, is the main office of the *Afro-American,* a newspaper founded by the late Carl Murphy (January 17, 1889–February 25, 1967). This man has given Black people their greatest public voice in the Baltimore-Washington-Richmond corridor, as part of liberation by publication. He was a strong devotee of prayer. After his death, his family collected some of his many prayers, and placed them in a booklet entitled *In Memoriam.* A sense of his spirit in prayer is caught in the following line:

> Send out Thy light that we can see,
> Send out the truth that we may avoid error
> And come to Thy Holy Hill where
> Freedom, Dignity, long denied
> Shall prevail at last.[19]

The Progressive National Baptist Convention, in its annual session meeting in Cleveland, Ohio, honored one of the leading publishers in the United States, John Harold Johnson, along with his mother, Mrs. Gertrude Williams. Johnson and his mother were presented the Martin Luther King Annual Award, September 13, by the convention. He was honored for his great accomplishments as a publisher and for his concern for the liberation of Black people through the printed word. His mother was honored for her great

[17] *Ibid.,* pp. 24-25.

[18] D. E. King, educator and clergyman, in an address, "Salute to Nannie Helen Burroughs," at Nannie Helen Burroughs School for Girls, Washington, D.C., July 9, 1973.

[19] Carl Murphy, *In Memorian* (Baltimore: Afro-American Newspapers, 1973), p. 19.

spiritual faith imparted so strongly in the life of her son. In his acceptance speech, Johnson stated:

> My mother used to take me to all-day services at church in Arkansas City, Arkansas. At church we all had to give our "determination." I didn't believe much in this practice then, but my mother's prayers and determination have now paid off. I believe we would do well to still build up that kind of faith in our young men and young women in today's world. A "determination" has a way of building character.[20]

It was revealed that Johnson's first $500, borrowed to start publication of the *Negro Digest,* came from his mother, who mortgaged her home to support a son. The sight of a praying mother and an accomplished son, sharing the platform together, gave living validity to the stream of Black prayers, meaningfully used in the liberation of Black people.

Nonviolence Through Prayer

The liberating relevance of the Black prayer tradition reached its modern-day summit in the heroic life and philosophy of Martin Luther King, Jr. During the days of his leadership, prayer was an integral part of every struggle, meeting, and decision.

In Montgomery, Alabama, the traditional prayer meeting served to bring together an oppressed people under a bold new philosophy, nonviolence based on Christian love. The songs of slavery came alive, matched with the thrust of spontaneous prayers for enemies and for freedom. Suddenly people of all colors and creeds began to take notice, as the prayers of former slave children were ringing out from jails, courthouses, streets, and churches.

King, in his own words, told how he prepared himself for his first speech in a mass prayer rally:

> I went to my study and closed the door. The minutes were passing fast. It was now six-thirty, and I had to leave no later than six-fifty to get to the meeting. This meant that I had only twenty minutes to prepare the most decisive speech of my life. As I thought of the limited time before me and the possible implications of this speech, I became possessed by fear. Each week I needed at least fifteen hours to prepare my Sunday sermon. Now I was faced with the inescapable task of preparing, in almost no time at all, a speech that was expected to give a sense of direction to a people imbued

[20] John H. Johnson, publisher of *Ebony, Jet,* and *Negro Digest* and president of the Johnson Publishing Company, Cleveland, September 13, 1974.

with a new and still unplumbed passion for justice. I was also conscious that reporters and television men would be there with their pencils and sound cameras poised to record my words and send them across the nation.

I was now almost overcome, obsessed by a feeling of inadequacy. In this state of anxiety, I had already wasted five minutes of the original twenty. With nothing left but faith in a power whose matchless strength stands over against the frailties and inadequacies of human nature, I turned to God in prayer. My words were brief and simple, asking God to restore my balance and to be with me in a time when I needed His guidance more than ever.

With less than fifteen minutes left, I began preparing an outline. In the midst of this, however, I faced a new and sobering dilemma: How could I make a speech that would be militant enough to keep my people aroused to positive action and yet moderate enough to keep this fervor within controllable and Christian bounds? I knew that many of the Negro people were victims of bitterness that could easily rise to flood proportions. What could I say to keep them courageous and prepared for positive action and yet devoid of hate and resentment? Could the militant and the moderate be combined in a single speech?

I decided that I had to face the challenge head on, and attempt to combine two apparent irreconcilables. I would seek to arouse the group to action by insisting that their self-respect was at stake and that if they accepted such injustices without protesting, they would betray their own sense of dignity and the eternal edicts of God Himself. But I would balance this with a strong affirmation of the Christian doctrine of love. By the time I had sketched an outline of the speech in my mind, my time was up. Without stopping to eat supper (I had not eaten since morning) I said good-by to Coretta and drove to the Holt Street Church.[21]

What a revealing account! The whole philosophy of nonviolence, based on the love ethic of Jesus Christ, became real to King in a moment of prayer! He credited much of his strength during those early days to the ever-fresh stream of prayer. His close associate, Ralph Abernathy, minister of the First Baptist Church of Montgomery, Alabama, was King's main prayer partner. "We prayed together and made important decisions together."[22]

During the early days of this hectic struggle, the threats against the life of King and his family had telling effects. One night in a mass meeting he said, "If one day you find me sprawled out dead, I do not want you to retaliate with a single act of violence. I urge you to

[21] Martin Luther King, Jr., *Stride Toward Freedom* (New York: Harper & Row, Publishers, 1958), pp. 59-60. Copyright © 1958 by Martin Luther King, Jr.
[22] *Ibid.*, p. 74.

continue protesting with the same dignity and discipline you have shown so far."[23]

> One night toward the end of January I settled into bed late, after a strenuous day. Coretta had already fallen asleep and just as I was about to doze off the telephone rang. An angry voice said, "Listen, nigger, we've taken all we want from you; before next week you'll be sorry you ever came to Montgomery." I hung up, but I couldn't sleep. It seemed that all of my fears had come down on me at once. I had reached the saturation point.
>
> I got out of bed and began to walk the floor. Finally I went to the kitchen and heated a pot of coffee. I was ready to give up. With my cup of coffee sitting untouched before me I tried to think of a way to move out of the picture without appearing a coward. In this state of exhaustion, when my courage had all but gone, I decided to take my problem to God. With my head in my hands, I bowed over the kitchen table and prayed aloud. The words I spoke to God that midnight are still vivid in my memory. "I am here taking a stand for what I believe is right. But now I am afraid. The people are looking to me for leadership, and if I stand before them without strength and courage, they too will falter. I am at the end of my powers. I have nothing left. I've come to the point where I can't face it alone."
>
> At that moment I experienced the presence of the Divine as I had never experienced Him before. It seemed as though I could hear the quiet assurance of an inner voice saying: "Stand up for righteousness, stand up for truth; and God will be at your side forever." Almost at once my fears began to go. My uncertainty disappeared. I was ready to face anything.[24]

King now felt the reassuring hand of God. His positive theme of nonviolence based on Christian love was preached with greater force. The familiar psalm of life, First Corinthians 13, became for Black people a watchword from God. The reading of this sacred passage often brought shouts of rejoicing in mass prayer meetings. Ralph Abernathy related how on one such occasion, a White reporter covering the prayer meeting observed the outburst on the part of the congregation to the psalm of life. "Isn't it a little peculiar," the journalist had asked, "for people to interrupt the Scripture in that way?"[25]

> "Yes it is," Abernathy quoted himself in reply. "Just as it is peculiar for people to walk in the snow and rain when there are empty buses available; just as it is peculiar for people to pray for those who persecute them; just as it is peculiar for the Southern Negro to stand up and look a

[23] *Ibid*, p. 133.
[24] *Ibid.*, pp. 134-135.
[25] *Ibid.*, p. 161.

white man in the face as an equal." At this his audience laughed and shouted and applauded.[26]

The sustaining power of prayer was an invaluable anchor when physical violence exploded. Abernathy's home was bombed. The Bell Street and Mount Olive Baptist churches were destroyed by fire. Things were looking mighty bad. King broke down in a prayer meeting.

> I had invited the audience to join me in prayer, and had begun by asking God's guidance and direction in all our activities. Then, in the grip of an emotion I could not control, I said, "Lord, I hope no one will have to die as a result of our struggle for freedom in Montgomery. Certainly I don't want to die. But if anyone has to die, let it be me." The audience was in an uproar. Shouts and cries of "no, no" came from all sides. So intense was the reaction, that I could not go on with my prayer. Two of my fellow ministers came to the pulpit and suggested that I take a seat. For a few minutes I stood with their arms around me, unable to move. Finally, with the help of my friends, I sat down. . . .
>
> Unexpectedly, this episode brought me great relief. Many people came up to me after the meeting and many called the following day to assure me that we were all together until the end.[27]

A similar episode occurred involving the successor of Dr. King, Ralph David Abernathy. The Poor People's Campaign in Washington was making its witness in Baltimore. Here Abernathy had addressed an overflowing mass prayer meeting at the New Shiloh Baptist Church. The strain on this man was unbelievable. After his lengthy message, which was received enthusiastically, he remained standing and burst into a spontaneous prayer with tears bathing his face:

> Oh God, it gets rough!
> No one knows what it is like out here . . .
> The burden and the pressures are heavy![28]

The writer remembers the pastoral prayers uttered by King when he pastored the Dexter Avenue Baptist Church, Montgomery, Alabama. The following prayer was typical.

> O God, our Heavenly Father, we thank thee for this golden privilege to worship thee, the only true God of the universe. We come to thee today,

[26] *Ibid.*, pp. 161-162.
[27] *Ibid.*, p. 178.
[28] Ralph Abernathy, in an address "Can't Turn Around Now," at New Shiloh Baptist Church, May 19, 1968.

grateful that thou hast kept us through the long night of the past and ushered us into the challenge of the present and the bright hope of the future. We are mindful, O God, that man cannot save himself, for man is not the measure of things and humanity is not God. Bound by our chains of sin and finiteness, we know we need a Savior. We thank thee, O God, for the spiritual nature of man. We are in nature but we live above nature. Help us never to let anyone or any condition pull us so low as to cause us to hate. Give us the strength to love our enemies and to do good to those who despitefully use us and persecute us. We thank thee for thy Church, founded upon thy Word, that challenges us to do more than sing and pray, but go out and work as though the very answer to our prayers depended on us and not upon thee. Then, finally, help us to realize that man was created to shine like the stars and live on through all eternity. Keep us, we pray, in perfect peace, help us to walk together, pray together, sing together, and live together until that day when all of God's children, Black, White, Red, and Yellow will rejoice in one common band of humanity in the kingdom of our Lord and of our God, we pray. Amen.[29]

The Black prayer tradition, so effectively used in the Montgomery bus boycott, was the rallying point for ministers and Christian laymen during later struggles for freedom and true brotherhood in Albany, Birmingham, Selma, and Washington, D.C. King issued calls from all of these cities for ministers to hold local prayer vigils against segregation and human injustice in local cities across the nation.

The Albany, Georgia, movement immediately witnessed the cohesiveness that the Black prayer tradition could generate.

The Albany venture had begun promisingly, and in keeping with the religious framework of King's ideas he had invited 75 Protestant, Jewish and Catholic laymen and clerics from around the U.S. to meet in Atlanta to support a prayer vigil for racial justice in Albany.

On a muggy afternoon shortly after, a convoy of cars drove up Pine Street in downtown Albany. "This looks like the Yankee preachers," murmured one bystander. Led by the Reverend Ralph Lord Roy, pastor of Manhattan's Grace Methodist Church, the group lined up in single file outside the city hall. Up stepped Laurie Pritchett, Albany's tough police chief. "All right, reverends," he said. "I want to know what your purpose is." Answered the Reverend Norman Eddy, of Manhattan's interracial East Harlem Protestant parish: "Our purpose is to offer our prayers to God."[30]

[29] Martin Luther King, in pastoral prayer at Dexter Avenue Baptist Church, Montgomery, Alabama, 1956.
[30] Charles Osborne, ed., *I Have a Dream* (New York: Time-Life Books, 1968), pp. 30-31.

A later struggle in Birmingham, Alabama, known as the harshest civil rights town in the South, produced a crisis of unparalleled proportions. Wyatt Tee Walker, a King lieutenant, stated, "We've got to have a crisis to bargain with. To take a moderate approach, hoping to get white help, doesn't work. They nail you to the cross, and it saps the enthusiasm of the followers. You've got to have a crisis." [31]

In such a crisis condition, a meaningful release valve was needed. A way was needed to vent long years of accumulated frustration, while maintaining a positive sense of direction. The Black prayer tradition was exactly the way. Wyatt Walker further stated that in Birmingham "all marchers left church inspired by a continuous flow of song and prayer before facing Bull Connor and his ruthless police dogs." [32] The result was seen in this descriptive passage of history:

> At length, on Tuesday, May 7 [1963], Negroes poured out of church, surged through the police lines and swarmed downtown. Connor furiously ordered the fire hoses turned on. Armed with clubs, cops beat their way into the crowds. In all, the Birmingham demonstrations resulted in the jailing of more than 3,300 Negroes, including King himself.[33]

The televised and widely reported scenes of Birmingham had great impact in mobilizing sit-in and kneel-in campaigns in major cities in the North as well as hundreds of new places in the South. Many Whites became involved in the struggle, particularly the White clergy. Suddenly ministers, priests, and rabbis were uniting forces around the old-time freedom prayers and the Black spiritual, "We Shall Overcome!" During those days, whenever persons were arrested for breaking unjust laws, traditional Black prayers were supporting their efforts.

James Forman was arrested for doing civil rights work among Black people in LeFlore County, Mississippi. He was comforted while in jail on hearing the ringing prayer of a Black woman outside.

> 12:30 p.m.: Sather of the Justice Department interviewed me about the events and while we were talking I heard some singing on the outside and our fellows yelling. Later we found out that 19 more people had been arrested. We sang and sang. There are five women in the cell next door. One old woman is now praying as the old folks pray in the South. Her voice has a musical quality as she appeals and prays to God, she is praying for

[31] *Time* magazine, vol. 83, no. 1 (January 3, 1964), p. 16.
[32] Wyatt Tee Walker, in a personal interview, Rochester, New York, July 20, 1974.
[33] Osborne, *op. cit.,* p. 38.

freedom in Greenwood, she is praying for mercy on Greenwood, she is praying for forgiveness in Greenwood, please she cries, go into the hospital, hold the church of God, you told us to love one another, there does not seem to be any love in this, look this town over Jesus and do something about the condition. Whatsoever a man soweth, that also shall he reap, that we might have our equal rights.[34]

The writer of this book was one of King's former associates and can recall similar experiences of prayer in the city of Lynchburg, Virginia. This conservative city, nestled in the hills of Virginia, had strong walls of segregation that needed to be torn down. On several occasions, White ministers heeded the call to join with Black ministers to pray in front of courthouses or in front of jails where protesters were held, making a witness for love and brotherhood. What we were doing in Lynchburg was happening in many cities around the country. The time was now ripe for a massive prayer pilgrimage to the nation's Capitol.

At noon on May 17, 1957, thirty-seven thousand marchers, including three thousand white sympathizers, assembled in front of the Lincoln Memorial. They were addressed by almost all the important black leaders of the day. It was about three o'clock when A. Philip Randolph introduced Martin to make the closing address. This was the first of Martin's inspiring political speeches to a national audience.[35]

The significance of this massive rally, billed as a "Prayer Pilgrimage," is at least fourfold. First, it brought together for the first time on a national platform the Southern Christian Leadership Conference and the National Association for the Advancement of Colored People. Second, it set the tone for the mammoth rally six years later, for which it was the indispensable rehearsal. Third, it provided a national and international platform for King to call the nation to repentance and sound justice. Fourth, it again proved the strength the Black prayer tradition had in providing for people from all walks of life a common anchor to pursue goals beneficial to all persons.

On August 28, 1963, a quarter of a million Americans of all colors gathered again in Washington, D.C., marching and singing the

[34] Joanne Grant, ed., *Black Protest* (Greenwich, Conn.: Fawcett Publications, Inc., 1968), pp. 333-334.
[35] Coretta Scott King, *My Life with Martin Luther King, Jr.* (New York: Holt, Rinehart and Winston, Inc., 1969), p. 159.

familiar song "We Shall Overcome!" Here King, true to the traditions of the past, spoke to the world with the spirit of his elders, "I Have a Dream!" His dream of true brotherhood, respect for human dignity, and the essential worth of all God's people, provided the Black prayer tradition one of its finest hours.

The rally just mentioned was designed also to call attention to the need of Black people for jobs and economic independence. This need has been tackled by Rev. Leon H. Sullivan, founder of the Opportunities Industrialization Center, Philadelphia, Pennsylvania. This program grew out of the Black community's efforts in Philadelphia to force businesses doing services in the Black community to return some of that investment to the community in the form of jobs and technical training. The campaign which lasted from 1959 through 1963 was known as a Selective Patronage campaign. One of the undergirding forces of this movement was prayer.

> To the four hundred colored ministers, prayer was an attempt constantly to identify a secular purpose with a heavenly cause. We believed that direction from God was indispensable if our goal was to be reached. We were attempting to do something that seemed to some impossible at that time of rigid segregation in industry, and we needed to be conscious of God's involvement and presence psychologically, spiritually and practically.[36]

Sullivan has guided the Opportunities Industrialization Center into being an international program for the training of nonemployed and underemployed workers. The slogan of this organization is "we help ourselves." The example set by this community-based program has elicited federal support. Recently this support was in danger of being cut off. Immediately, Sullivan issued a call for ministers and concerned workers to make "a pilgrimage of hope, a journey of sacred purpose," and an all-night prayer vigil was held on the steps of the nation's Capitol March 28, 1973, beginning at 11:00 P.M., continuing through the night until 11:00 A.M. the following day. The federal support did come, and the program of skill training continues for those persons needing it, without regard to race, creed, or color.

[36] Leon H. Sullivan, *Build Brother Build* (Philadelphia: Macrae Smith Company, 1969), pp. 77-78.

A more recent illustration of the Black prayer tradition serving the cause of liberation for Black people in economics comes from Jesse Jackson, founder and president of PUSH.[37] He called together a summit meeting of Black clergymen to address them about the task of the Black church, to witness as one voice in the economic, social, and spiritual redemption of Black people in America.

This meeting opened with a period of prayer, and after a full morning's session of wrestling with major issues confronting Black people and the peoples of America generally, Jesse Jackson arose to make some closing remarks.

> My brethren, you all know I was a vital part of the civil rights struggle under the leadership of Martin Luther King. One of the problems we faced was whether our struggle was social or spiritual. We were constantly faced with the problem of whether the church should be in politics or stay out of politics. We must not let this be our problem. We need both prayer and political and social power. All that we have as a people came essentially through prayer, through spiritual power, and the application of this power to life. Let us therefore bow our heads and spend these closing minutes in prayer. Brethren, we need the presence of God in our efforts.[38]

The brethren assembled bowed their heads and were led in prayer by M. C. Williams. In his prayer he sought to remind us how God had brought us along life's way, and he challenged us to remain firmly committed to this God who alone could strengthen our will and provide for us a way.

Negro National Anthem—A Model Prayer

There is a prayer, originally written by James Weldon Johnson to celebrate Abraham Lincoln's birthday in 1900, that Black people use in all kinds of major functions as a kind of Negro national anthem. Specifically, the words were written for a group of young men in Jacksonville, Florida. Johnson never dreamed this song would be adopted by so many Black people and spread throughout the land. Surely this result occurred because the closing words of this anthem express the general prayers of Black people in every walk of life.

[37] PUSH is a national civil rights organization founded by Jesse Jackson in Chicago, Illinois. The very letters mean People United to Save Humanity. Historically, PUSH is an outgrowth of the Southern Christian Leadership Conference economic base program to secure jobs, employment, and freedom for minority people in Chicago, Illinois. The organization was founded during the year 1968.

[38] Jesse Jackson, Ministers' Summit Meeting, Chicago, Illinois, September 27, 1974.

God of our weary years,
God of our silent tears,
Thou who hast brought us thus far on the way,
Thou who hast by Thy might
Led us into the light,
Keep us forever in the path, we pray;
Lest our feet stray from the places, our God,
    where we met Thee,
Lest, our hearts drunk with the wine of the
    world, we forget Thee . . .
Shadowed beneath Thy hand, may we forever stand
True to our God, true to our Native Land.[39]

Johnson described his emotions when he wrote this poem:

I could not keep back the tears, and made no effort to do so. I was experiencing the transports of the poet's ecstasy. Feverish ecstasy was followed by that contentment—that sense of serene joy—which makes artistic creation the most complete of all human experiences.

When I had put the last stanza down on paper I at once recognized the Kiplingesque touch in the two longer lines quoted above; but I knew that in the stanza the American Negro was, historically and spiritually, immanent; and I decided to let it stand as it was written.[40]

This prayer is a model prayer for many reasons. It embraces the concerns and elicits the allegiance of the Black community, regardless of denominational affiliation or cultural status. In beautiful language it expresses a prayer in the authentic African and Black-American view of God and humanity. It gives profound credit to God for our past and our present, and it looks to God for our future. It faces the plight we have come through and calls on us to be vigilant against the "wine of the world." Above all, it calls upon us to be "True to our God, true to our Native Land."

In this chapter we have seen the genius of the Black prayer tradition at work. It has been used by Black women to provide hope and the value of freedom in the hearts of their children. Slaves used this tradition to free themselves and to seek the freedom of other slaves left behind. This prayer tradition provided the spiritual strength for the Black community to sustain a nonviolent struggle against segregation and oppression during the civil rights movement. It

[39] James Weldon Johnson, *Along This Way* (New York: Da Capo Press, 1933), p. 155.
[40] *Ibid.*

provided a kind of spiritual umbrella for national civic organizations to plan the mass prayer pilgrimage on Washington, resulting in more jobs for Black people and the right to use the ballot. It has proved itself to be a source of power, not locked behind stained-glass windows, but used wherever Black people seek God's will and respond to his way. It is seen in the closing stanza of "The Negro National Anthem" as a prayer to which all Black people can relate, regardless of cultural status or religious affiliation. In the chapter following, we shall see how this Black prayer tradition can go on serving as an ongoing model of creative spiritual power.

7

The Black Prayer Tradition— An Ongoing Model

People are finite and will always need to pray. Some things are changed, others improved; still others call for new styles. Prayer in Black culture is hardly a matter of passing fancy although it has been responsive to the deep and changing needs of Black people. It is still one of their basic ways of finding meaning and personhood in life. The fact of black skin color has caused repressive reactions in many areas of their life. Black people still seek the dream of a beloved community, where everyone is judged solely by the character of one's life and not by the pigment of one's skin. The Black person, therefore, needs the traditional strength of Black prayers to provide meaning from the past, affirmation for the present, and hope for the future. The creative prayer meeting can still fulfill this need when its power is released in songs, words, prayers, and testimonies. The following discussion will propose some ideas of how the creative prayer meeting can be developed in today's world.

Creative Prayer

The African and Afro-American sensitivity to the presence of God is not only a means of access to spiritual power, but it also builds persons by providing acceptance and openness to God's work in each person. This has been the strength that the traditional Black prayer meeting has used. It must still be the strength! No formal order of worship has ruled this meeting. No absolute observance of time has dictated when one should pray or how long one should pray. The order of this service has followed the responses of the persons involved in worship.

There is strength to be derived from this tradition. This spontaneous way of having prayer meetings gives opportunity for any person to be prayer leader. This does not usurp the minister's role. True, the minister ought to attend prayer meetings and become deeply involved. But he ought to recognize the power of this hour to provide creative leadership and growth for people, young and old.

The creative prayer meeting must always be sensitive and responsive to the powers of living imagination. We have seen how this ability to make words and actions real during prayer has sustained the hopes of Black people. It should be remembered that "the only guarantee that a subject is theoretically coherent is its ability to have its elementary principles taught to children."[1] This has been the secret of the Black prayer meeting's ongoing life. The everyday drama of an otherwise meaningless life is lifted into significance as Black people dialogue with God in prayer.

> Whether or not written in the form of dialogue, works focusing on the everyday life of moderate men are seldom "dramatic," as they tend to lack intensity, suspense, surprise, reversal, and other dramatic qualities.[2]

Yet when we recognize that in the Black prayer meeting the hero becomes anyone who commits one's life fully to the hand of God, then we see how drama becomes a part of this experience.

> "The great turn of the wheel of fortune which carries the hero to the extremes of joy and grief, often in one moment of dazzling intensity, is the dramatic symbol of the endless little ups and downs, the little sorrows and

[1] Northrop Frye, "The Developing Imagination" in *Learning in Language and Literature* (Cambridge: Harvard University Press, 1963), p. 33.

[2] Paul Hernadi, *Beyond Genre, New Directions in Literary Classification* (Ithaca, N.Y.: Cornell University Press, 1972), p. 94. Copyright © 1972 by Cornell University.

joys, of ordinary men." In other words, drama does not falsify or distort life; it projects certain elements in life to a larger, more visible screen.[3]

This is the end which the creative prayer meeting must always seek. Each person in this setting can be an authentic hero acting out one's life before God and others. Here one's words have ultimate meaning and one's acts are supported and authenticated by the larger congregation.

Philip Wheelwright helps us to understand better the many forces at work in imagination. He argues that there are four ways people may imagine. They are confrontative imagining, imaginative distancing, metaphoric imagining, and archetypal imagining.[4] In confrontative imagination we experience a person or God face to face. We break through all the technological and bureaucratic forces in our lives and find meaning through direct acquaintance with another person, even with God. The language of the creative prayer meeting is needed in our times to overcome the tendency to reduce humans to things and God to an impersonal object. Men and women still need a face-to-face experience with God and with one another!

In "imaginative distancing," the worshiper keeps in sight that God is still holy and persons are still of infinite worth. This aspect of imagination at work in the creative prayer meeting would guard against the temptation to make God a casual acquaintance or even to forget the proper respect for persons.

In the next aspect of imagination, "compositive imagining," the worshiper finds a balance, a reconcilement of the opposite and discordant qualities of life. Here the words of prayer are used to bring healing, to make for wholeness.

The helter-skelter quality of modern-day life is desperately in need of a harmonizing power. The creative and poetic prayer language of traditional Black prayers could serve this need, providing a healing station to prove there is "Balm in Gilead to make the wounded whole."[5]

"Archetypal imagining," while combining much of the other three, goes on to find meaning in a higher or deeper order than itself. It is

[3] Ibid.

[4] Philip Wheelwright, *The Burning Fountain* (Bloomington, Ind.: Indiana University Press, 1954), pp. 76-100.

[5] Line from a traditional Black spiritual, based on the question of Jeremiah, the prophet of God. See Jeremiah 8:22.

aware that imagination is finally meaningless unless it points the way to God. Thus, in the creative Black prayer meeting, only three or four persons may be present, but their acts take on universal significance. Their words filled with powerful prayer imaginations are not empty but are strivings enriching their lives and relating them to the Rock of their salvation, even God, the Father of all mankind.

This type of creative prayer meeting is never regimented to a particular arrangement of song, word, or prayer. What is important is the ability to respond to the sense of the guiding presence of God. The songs and the prayers ought to be given voluntarily, as much as possible. The congregation ought to feel free to move with the spirit. The leader of the prayer meeting ought to be enthusiastic without being overbearing. She or he must remember that she or he is there to lead others to make their own approach to the throne of God.

Every church would do well to provide some definite hour for prayer when members are vigorously urged to come out and participate in this service. In this hour, songs of the spirit can burst out anew from the worshiping souls of God's people. God's word can be taught to enrich the experience of prayer. The altar call can be used not merely to provide spiritual blessings, but also to call persons to specific tasks of evangelistic and civic development.

The Creative Word

Memorization seems a virtue of the past. Why have modern men and women failed to memorize some of the meaningful passages of Scripture? They have not been challenged to do so. The traditional prayers of Black people reflect a strong influence from the Bible, God's Holy Word. The Black person, today, must return to the serious study of God's words. The prayer meeting is an excellent time to do this.

Spontaneous prayer can come only from lips accustomed to speaking words about God and his people. Inescapably, to do so requires a memorized body of oral traditional materials to provide vocabulary. Rich prayer is kindled with biblical knowledge. Knowing the rich promises of God in Scripture always provides a relevant stand on which one can plead before God. There is also the sense of glory and thanksgiving arising out of God's Word. Through the study of God's Word, and the informal and natural immersion in biblical ideas and language, the spirit of prayer will come alive in ways the human tongue cannot fully explain.

The Creative "Hymn Book"

It is not necessary for worshipers to gaze at the hymn book each time a song is sung. Yet this is what modern people tend to do! They have become unconsciously dependent in worship. They have lost sight of the upward flow of the soul to God.

Past generations sang praises unto God without books, out of necessity, and as a result left us a golden heritage of song. The Black person today must recapture the creative flow and sing anew the hymns known in the book and felt in the soul, as expressions of praise to God. This act will provide a new dimension to the prayer meeting.

The spontaneous expression of song parallels the needed flow of fresh words of prayer, and the prayer meeting which unlocks this flow is recovering the source-springs of profound, people-empowering folk religion.

Worshipers must be willing to take the risk of being creative. We must not conclude that the last hymn has been written and the last folk song recorded. The fresh joy of spontaneous song creation is uniquely suited for prayer meetings. The Black prayer tradition did just this with slave spirituals and their adaptation for civil rights purposes. This still can be done in any church where Black people are encouraged to sing out of depths of sincerity, measured only by the light of Christ.

The Black prayer tradition must seek anew to learn from men like Thomas A. Dorsey, commonly called the "Father of Gospel Music," who permitted the natural flow of his soul to produce one of the greatest of all prayerful songs, "Precious Lord, Take My Hand." Dorsey was asked, "How did you come to write 'Precious Lord'?" He answered:

"Precious Lord" came twisting out of my very heart because of the death of a dear one. A songwriter . . . and I were scheduled to go out of town to sing at a revival meeting. My wife—my first wife, Nettie [Harper]—was in the late days of a pregnancy. . . . The next night at the revival meeting, they brought me a telegram. The baby was doing fine. But my wife had been lost down in the valley and the shadow of death.

I found myself stumbling up on some new words which suited my mood of dejection and despair: *Precious Lord—take my hand. Lead me on. Let me stand. I am tired.* True, I was so tired. *I am weak. I am worn. Through the storm.* Plenty storm in my life now. *Through the night.* Hard night. *Lead me on to the light.* . . . *Precious Lord. Take my hand. Lead me on.*

The words were so simple. It was a simple song, but it came right out of me almost as if God had personally dictated every syllable.[6]

Every Black person may not give the world a prayerful song like "Precious Lord," but he or she can be open to God's spirit. One can be open so that one's total life can be used to create in a unique way a new note in the total melody of life.

The Creative Conquering of Fear of Prayer

The first emotion regarding prayer in public is usually fear. Even the best of speakers has known fear. This fear is overcome initially in small groups, where feelings are reasonably relaxed and expectations not exceedingly high. However, prayer is never to be judged, but rather to be received and shared. Prayer is not a display of knowledge; it is a sharing of one's deep desires with God and with the extended family of prayer. In this medium, prayer can be an enriching experience, strengthening the witness of the timid and humbling the arrogant and the proud.

Pastoral leadership is definitely required to arrange and provide for orderly growth toward courage in prayer witness. Such growth. may not happen if left to chance. A whole new breed of sensitive, creative lay leaders may be needed to teach and counsel toward a renewed and relevant Black prayer tradition. These lay leaders ought to catch their vision from the minister in song, in word, and in prayer, and share it with their families and those about them.

Creative Sentence Prayers and Testimonies

The Mount Sinai Holy Church of Philadelphia can teach us something about the power of sentence prayers. This church has a way of permitting members to stand at will, with many or few on the floor, and utter their petitions to God. This is a genuine worship experience.

This act of worship has repeatedly been done in the New Shiloh

[6] Alfred Duckett, "An Interview with Thomas A. Dorsey," *Black World,* vol. 23, no. 9 (July, 1974), pp. 13-14. Copyright © July, 1974, by *Black World.* Reprinted by permission.

Baptist Church, Baltimore, Maryland. The response is always amazing. First, the sound of people at prayer is strangely holy. Second, we believe in an omnipresent and omniscient God. Such a God can hear all his creatures who pray. Third, this opportunity opens the way for the weak and the strong to pray without the eye of the congregation gazing upon any particular person.

This form of prayer does not rule out the practical advantage of having sentence prayers one at a time. This form of prayer needs not be eternal to be immortal.[7] It lifts people from the habit of rote prayers, and it causes them to say in one or two lines exactly the thought they would utter to God.

Also the old-fashioned testimony service is still around, begging for constructive use. When we recount how the messages of Scripture are essentially testimonies of God's people, how he dealt with them, and how they made it through life, then we receive a new appreciation for the testimonies of God's people today, who are indeed a part of the living Bible.

The leader of worship must not let one or two persons, who normally seek to control these open services, destroy their effectiveness. Once the leader has stated the framework of the meeting and suggested some time guideline, he or she has license gently to stop persons who would overdo such a service. Moreover, persons can be guided in their testimonies, holding the messages to specific concerns. For example, persons could testify on what it means to tithe, to trust God in the rearing of children, or to trust God as a healer. The subjects are endless, and some planning could give creative glow to this service.

Creative Prayers of Youth

Planting the desire of prayer in the hearts of children is extremely important. Their expressions in prayer are real and sometimes startling. They seek the opportunity to lend their spirits, as only their unspoiled attitudes and experience in life will admit.

In a Saturday church school program at the New Shiloh Baptist Church, Baltimore, Maryland, time is given weekly for children, ages six to fourteen, to pray. Two basic trends emerge from this experience. First, some have prayers given to them by parents or

[7] In Matthew 6:7-8, Jesus warns against the futility of long prayers.

teachers. Secondly, others pray as they are moved. There is virtue in both practices. Parents and teachers ought to instruct children in prayer but then permit children to develop their own responses in body and spirit before God. The following two prayers are typical of ones that are spoken by the youth in New Shiloh:

> Dear God, bless my mother, my father, my teachers, and my friends. Thank you for our Saturday church school. Help me to be like Jesus. Amen.[8]

> Lord, there is so much sin in our world, and you told us to live right and love one another. Please help me to be a better person. Help me to let my light shine for Jesus. Bless my parents, my sisters and my brothers, my pastor, and my teachers, and bless all of my friends, I pray. Amen.[9]

The abiding strength of the Black prayer tradition and the way it influences Black youth are even more encouraging when found in intellectual circles. Such is the case with Barbara Hendricks, who finds prayer to be an intimate part of her sudden rise to fame as a soprano soloist. Ms. Hendricks is the daughter of a Methodist district superintendent in Little Rock, Arkansas, and is a graduate from the University of Nebraska, with a major in chemistry and mathematics. While studying in college, she had a sideline job of singing in a jazz band. This sideline musical interest eventually brought her to Juilliard School of Music, New York City. Recently, Ms. Hendricks was called to learn the title role in Cavalli's *Calisto* in less than three weeks, as a substitute for a stricken soprano, and to perform at the Glyndebourne Festival in England. She states that her own "case of hay fever [was] ameliorated by prayer and a lot of Vitamin C." She went on to register an important triumph and is currently singing with the Chicago Symphony Orchestra. "Praying comes as natural to Hendricks as singing."[10]

The naturalness of prayer was demonstrated by Johnathan Jones, seventeen years of age, in an afternoon musical service in a Baptist church in Baltimore. Johnathan prayed the traditional prayer of Black people, as though he had been around when it first surfaced on the anvil of Black folk experiences. The listener could not escape

---

[8] Prayer by Wanda Jones, eight years old, Saturday church school, New Shiloh Baptist Church, Baltimore, Maryland, January, 1974.

[9] Prayer by Robert Evans, eleven years of age, Saturday church school, New Shiloh Baptist Church, Baltimore, Maryland, March, 1974.

[10] *People* magazine, vol. 2, no. 12 (Sept. 16, 1974), p. 43.

some sense of satisfaction that the Black experiences of the past, transmitted in the prayer, were giving meaning to Black youth as they carve out their places and make their contributions to today's world.

The Creative Altar Call

All persons hearing the Word of God are called upon to make some commitment. God's Word always calls, and people cannot escape some response. Either the response will be negative, degenerating into no action, no involvement, or positive, leading forth to greater service for Christ.

Since the need to respond is present, the altar call serves the role of enlistment and involvement. Its emphasis ought to be the calling forth of the best virtues in people.

It is not enough for persons to seek always to receive a blessing. They must make a commitment for positive community service. Each church could keep an accurate, up-to-date listing of persons who might be unchurched and without Christ. Various legislators who might be defaulting on constructive community bills could also be contacted and prodded into supporting meaningful laws for the total community. Unjust government or business structures could be on this list, providing for persons who come to the altar an opportunity to go and make a witness with the strong backing of the church. Commitments could be made at the altar, by persons able and willing to do so, to serve the special needs of families or children.

This discussion of the creative Black prayer meeting ought to make us aware that it is not dead but is suffering from the lack of use. Afro-Americans have a religious attitude that greatly equips them for sharing in open prayer meetings. Their sense of the presence of God and their desire to share in this presence through prayer help to build community and create viable lay leadership. The Black church today must recapture the important emphasis the prayer meeting has known in the past. To do this, the Black pastor must provide personal leadership in this service. He must be willing and anxious to teach God's Word, an all-important ingredient in influencing prayer language and prayer expectations. The spontaneous flow of creative song must be recaptured, rebuilding the sense of folk religion, where everyone can feel an important part in the religious process. In this prayer meeting, no one will look down upon another. The guiding rule will be sincerity, as measured in the light of Christ. Everyone will have opportunity to pray, and everyone will be challenged to commit one's life to going forth into the community to perform some service beneficial to the commonweal of all people.

This is what this study is all about. It is about a people who found joy in spontaneous prayer meetings that enriched and gave meaning to their lives and that provided meaning and personhood for the lives of their children and unborn generations. The Black prayer meeting today recognizes that the prayers of the preacher and all the saints are needed if this old world is to be a better place in which to live. The book is written with the hope that it will call forth a new and genuine appreciation of the Black prayer tradition, its legacy, its strength, and its abiding values.

8

Summary and Conclusion

The Afro-American tradition in prayer deserves due recognition, because of the major contribution it has provided in the total development of Black people. The slaves were deeply involved in prayer and song in praise houses long before any organized missionary thrust sought to Christianize them. Prayer colored their total existence and was not merely an escape from reality. They knew that God had acted in history and delivered Israel from bondage in Egypt. And so they sang, "Go down, Moses, way down in Egypt's land, tell ol' Pharaoh to let my people go." [1] The slaves saw themselves as being in Egypt. God had now chosen them as his "New Israel," and God alone would provide deliverance. Therefore, secret prayer meetings in the fields of the Southland, making use of pots turned upside down, supposedly to catch the sound and prevent the master from hearing, were not meetings devoid of purpose and content. To

[1] Traditional Black folk spiritual.

the contrary, the slaves prayed for conversion in these meetings. They prayed for freedom and for a better day for their children.

Something important happened in these meetings. A folk theology was born that gave foundation to prayers and provided the biblical undergirding that made the Black prayer tradition the historic force that it is. God became for them the supreme ruler of heaven and earth, and he could do anything but fail. God was the one who acted in the lives of the fathers and would not default on their prayers and faithfulness to him, nor in the lives of their sons and daughters. Therefore, the fathers must be venerated and spiritually respected for their contributions in life. Just as God spoke through the fathers, he will now speak through the sons. Moreover, as God speaks to people, he always has some special person who can deliver his word. For the Black people, that person is God's prophet. The minister who prays is seen in prophetic light. He speaks not his word, but he speaks under the unction and guidance of the Holy Spirit.

The place where God's Holy Spirit is supremely felt and shared is the church. Jesus, the Son of God, is the founder and absolute ruler of the church. Jesus is not some theological figure over whom endless theological debates occur as to his nature. Jesus is the Savior who "is a-listening, to hear somebody pray." [2] Jesus is the one who "rides all the time." He rides into sick rooms, hospitals, jail houses, wherever people need him. He heals the sick and provides courage for the feeble. He is the One who permits every burdened spirit to pray her "every tribulation into manageable size." [3]

The devil is real in this tradition, but his power is limited by the hand of God. The devil seeks the destruction of one's soul and seeks to keep one from prayer. "He is a liar and a deceiver, too, and if you don't watch out, he'll conquer you." The only way to watch out for the devil is to rebuke him in Jesus' name.

Thus, Black people keep a note of praise in their hearts. Times may be bad and the problems in life may be heavy, but they believe in praising God anyhow! The Black person is able to say, "It's another day's journey, and I'm so glad; the devil couldn't do me no harm." He or she thanks the Lord for "waking me up this morning and starting

[2] Traditional Black folk spiritual.
[3] Maya Angelou, *Gather Together in My Name* (New York: Random House, 1974), p. 181.

me on my way." The Black person says, "Lord, have mercy," to practically any experience in life. Black people have a reserved way of feeling that things could have been worse; so they go through life "thanking God for my time."

Along this prayer-filled road, the Black prayer tradition has given birth to churches, developed church leaders, provided a pathway for female leadership, and proved itself a healing ground for physical, mental, and spiritual diseases. The historic development of Black churches in the urban North is really a record of how prayer meetings started in someone's home or a rented hall, and from these beginnings an established church developed. This informal prayer tradition also provided the cohesive spiritual experience from the revival fires of the South to the cold and industrial attitudes of the North. Here Black women could form their own prayer bands and minister in the community. Here religious leaders of all types could declare their blessings at the end of a praying line. It is a fact of history that Black people responded in larger numbers to those churches where traditional Black prayers were prayed, and the congregation was freely and fully involved.

Without monetary or political power, Black people still found through prayer a creative release for their frustrations. They learned how to take their burdens to the Lord and leave them there. They knew the power of a song freely wedded to a prayer, and they concluded that when one was too despondent to speak, one could still moan. Their desire was to make it through life "with no visible marks of God's displeasure upon them."[4]

Were the Black prayer tradition not intimately associated with the liberation struggles of Black people, then the critics of prayer could rightly accuse it of being a pious flight from reality. Indeed, the liberation march of Black people in education, publication, and civil rights owes its strength to the genius of Black prayers. The question could seriously be debated whether Martin Luther King, Jr., might have led a sustained nonviolent struggle against racial oppression without the historic conditioning of the Black prayer tradition upon the lives of Black people.

Reinhold Niebuhr, writing some years before the coming of Martin Luther King, stated:

[4] Traditional Black prayer line.

The technique of non-violence will not eliminate all these perils. But it will reduce them. . . . One waits for such a campaign with all the more reason and hope because the peculiar spiritual gifts of the Negro endow him with the capacity to conduct it successfully. He would need only to fuse the aggressiveness of the new and young Negro with the patience and forbearance of the old Negro, to rob the former of its vindictiveness and the latter of its lethargy.[5]

Martin Luther King, Jr., brought this prophetic utterance to pass as he seized the latent spiritual gifts of Black people and made Black prayers central to his civic thrust. The flexibility of this prayer tradition made prayer relevant for Black people during the civil rights movement, in jails, in the streets, before courthouses, and even in the nation's Capitol. This tradition must be credited with bringing together Black people from all ranks and stations in life, supporting causes for the good of all men, without regard to race, creed, or color. Each time the "Negro National Anthem" is sung, the singer is really uttering a prayer, without denominational or social status designation, that he or she will be "true to our God, true to our Native Land."

If indeed Black people are going to be true to God and to their "native land," they must no longer take the Black prayer tradition for granted. The folk wells of creative inspiration that gave birth to Black songs and prayer show signs of being polluted and withered with the lack of serious concern. The Black pastor must respond to this loss and generate new emphasis in the traditional Black prayer meeting. A whole new generation of Black lay leaders must be developed to carry on this powerful prayer tradition, providing strength and spiritual power for generations of tomorrow.

There is a solid basis for optimism about the ongoing force of Black prayers. This optimism is grounded in the innate God-consciousness of Black people and their general disposition to be responsive to the Spirit of God. It is grounded in the ongoing fact of Black liberation struggles and the need to wed present causes for brotherhood and social justice to spiritual gems in prayers and songs from the distant past. Such a wedding occurred during the recent civil rights movement when the Black spiritual "We Shall Overcome" became a rallying ground for all people who seek freedom, justice, and

[5] Reinhold Niebuhr, *Moral Man and Immoral Society* (New York: Charles Scribner's Sons, 1932), p. 254.

brotherhood. Innately linked to this renowned slave hymn is the slave prayer. Since it is not tied to the book but depends on the spirit, it is capable of utterance anywhere. It has a word of hope for the lonely, a word of peace for the warring, and a word of love for all. Its nature is akin to the words of Jesus. "The wind bloweth where it listeth, and thou hearest the sound thereof but canst not tell whence it cometh, and whither it goeth" (John 3:8, KJV). So it is with the power of Black prayers. Since these prayers are rooted in an unseen Source, it doth not yet appear to us what may be the full magnitude of their power. For Black people to forsake this heritage would be to deny a life-producing stream that would, in turn, rob humanity of a people who share an intimate prayer romance with God.

Bibliography

Magazine, monthly:

Black World, vol. 22, no. 9, July, 1974.

Ebony magazine, November, 1973.

People magazine, September 16, 1974.

Reader's Digest, vol. 105, no. 629, September, 1974.

Time magazine, vol. 83, no. 1, January 3, 1964.

Newspaper, city:

Afro-American newspaper (Baltimore), October 6, 1973; November 6, 1973; August 24, 1974.

The News American (Baltimore), November, 1973.

Single volume works:

Angelou, Maya, *Gather Together in My Name.* New York: Random House, 1974.

——, *I Know Why the Caged Bird Sings.* New York: Bantam Books, 1969.

Baldwin, James, *The Fire Next Time.* New York: The Dial Press, 1963.

Bradford, Sarah H., *Scenes in the Life of Harriet Tubman.* Auburn: W. J. Moses, Printer, 1869.

Cable, Mary, *Black Odyssey.* New York: The Viking Press, 1971.

Courlander, Harold, *Tales of Yoruba Gods and Heroes.* Connecticut: Fawcett World, Inc., 1974.

Douglass, Frederick, *Life and Times of Frederick Douglass.* New York: Crowell-Collier and Macmillan, Inc., 1962.

Doyle, Bertram, *The Etiquette of Race Relations in the South.* Port Washington, N.Y.: Kennikat Press, Inc., 1968.

Fauset, Arthur Huff, *Black Gods of the Metropolis.* Philadelphia: University of Pennsylvania Press, 1971.

——, *Sojourner Truth: God's Faithful Pilgrim.* Chapel Hill: University of North Carolina Press, 1938.

Fisher, Miles Mark, *Negro Slave Songs in the United States.* New York: Cornell University Press, 1953.

Foner, Eric, ed., *America's Black Past: A Reader in Afro-American History.* New York: Harper & Row, Publishers, 1970.

Frazier, E. Franklin, *The Negro Church in America.* New York: Schocken Books, Inc., 1966.

Frye, Northrop, "The Developing Imagination," in *Learning in Language and Literature.* Cambridge: Harvard University Press, 1963.

Georgia Writers' Project, Works Project Administration, *Drums and Shadows!* Athens: University of Georgia Press, 1940.

Grant, Joanne, ed., *Black Protest.* Greenwich, Conn.: Fawcett Publications, Inc., 1968.

Gray, Thomas C., *The Confessions of Nat Turner, Leader of the Late Insurrection in Southampton, Va.* Miami: Mnemosyne Publishing Inc., 1969.

Hamilton, Charles V., *The Black Preacher in America.* New York: William Morrow & Company, Inc., 1972.

Hernadi, Paul, *Beyond Genre: New Directions in Literary Classification,* Ithaca, N.Y.: Cornell University Press, 1972.

Johnson, Charles, *Growing Up in the Black Belt.* Washington, D.C.: American Council on Education, 1941.

Johnson, Clifton H., ed., *God Struck Me Dead.* Philadelphia: Pilgrim Press, 1969.

Johnson, James Weldon, *Along This Way.* New York: Da Capo Press, Inc., 1933.

King, Coretta Scott, *My Life with Martin Luther King, Jr.* New York: Holt, Rinehart and Winston, 1969.

King, Martin Luther, Jr., *Stride Toward Freedom.* New York: Harper & Row, Publishers, 1958.

Lovell, John, Jr., *Black Song: The Forge and the Flame.* New York: The Macmillan Company, 1972.

Matthews, Basil, *Booker T. Washington.* Cambridge: Harvard University Press, 1948.

Mays, Benjamin E., *The Negro's God.* New York: Atheneum Publishers, 1969.

Mays, Benjamin E., and Nicholson, Joseph W., *The Negro's Church.* New York: Russell & Russell Publishers, 1969.

Mbiti, John S., *African Religions and Philosophy.* New York: Praeger Publishers, Inc., 1971.

Metcalf, George R., *Black Profiles.* New York: McGraw-Hill Book Co., 1970.

Murphy, Carl, *In Memoriam.* Baltimore: Afro-American Press, 1963.

Nichols, Charles H., *Black Men in Chains: Narratives by Escaped Slaves.* New York: Lawrence Hill & Company, 1972.

Niebuhr, Reinhold, *Moral Man and Immoral Society.* New York: Charles Scribner's Sons, 1932.

Osborne, Charles, ed., *I Have a Dream.* New York: Time-Life Books, 1968.

Ottenberg, Simon and Phoebe, *Cultures and Societies of Africa.* New York: Random House, Inc., 1964.

Puckett, Newbell Niles, *Folk Beliefs of the Southern Negro.* Chapel Hill, N.C.: University of North Carolina Press, 1926.

Rawick, George P., *The American Slave: A Composite Autobiography.* Westport, Conn.: Greenwood Publishing Company, 1972. Vols. 1, 6, 10, 18.

Reddy, John, "Making of a Champion." *Reader's Digest,* vol. 105, September, 1974, p. 45.

Rosenberg, Bruce A., *The Art of the American Folk Preacher.* New York: Oxford University Press, 1970.

Smith, Alvin D., *George Washington Carver, Man of God.* Middletown, Ohio: Perry Printing Co., 1961.

Smith, Charles Spencer, *A History of the African Methodist Episcopal Church.* Philadelphia: Book Concern of the A.M.E. Church, 1922.

Spear, Allan H., *Black Chicago.* Chicago: The University of Chicago Press, 1967.

Stearn, Charles, *Narrative of Henry Box Brown.* Boston: Brown & Stearn, 1849.

Sullivan, Leon H., *Build Brother Build.* Philadelphia: Macrae Smith Company, 1969.

Thurman, Howard, *Deep River.* New York: Harper & Row, Publishers, 1955.

_____, *The Luminous Darkness.* New York: Harper & Row, Publishers, 1965.

Washington, Joseph R., Jr., *Black Sects and Cults.* New York: Doubleday & Company, Inc., 1972.

————, *The Politics of God: The Future of the Black Churches.* Boston: Beacon Press, 1969.

Wheelwright, Philip, *The Burning Fountain.* Bloomington: Indiana University Press, 1954.

Wilmore, Gayraud S., *Black Religion and Black Radicalism.* New York: Doubleday & Company, Inc., 1972.

Woodson, Carter G., *The History of the Negro Church.* Washington, D.C.: Associated Publishers, 1921.

**Multivolume works,
individual volume:**

Hughes, Langston, and Bontemps, Arna, eds., *Book of Negro Folklore.* New York: Dodd, Mead & Co., 1958.

The International Library of Negro Life and History. 10 vols. Philadelphia: United Publishing Corp., 1970.

Unpublished sources

Abernathy, Ralph David, address heard by the writer. Baltimore. May 19, 1968.

Jackson, Jesse, address heard by the writer. PUSH. Chicago, Illinois. September 27, 1974.

Johnson, John H., address heard by the writer. Progressive National Baptist Convention. Cleveland, Ohio. September 13, 1974.

King, D. E., address heard by the writer. Washington, D.C. July 9, 1973.

————, unpublished sermons heard by the writer. Baltimore, Maryland. 1973.

King, Martin Luther, Jr., heard by the writer. Montgomery. 1955.

————, heard by the writer. Montgomery. 1956.

Prayer and Radio Ministry Letters, New Shiloh Baptist Church. Baltimore, Maryland. 1973.

Washington, C. L., personal letter to the writer. Washington, D.C. October, 1973.

"The World's Most Amazing Prophet Bishop," letter received by the writer. February, 1974.

Bartlett, Gene, personal interview. Chicago, Illinois. March, 1974.

Jackson, Joseph, personal interview. Chicago, Illinois. April, 1974.

Jones, William A., Jr., personal interview. Rochester, New York, July, 1974.

———, personal interview. Rochester, New York, August 24, 1974.

McKinney, Samuel Berry, personal interview. Rochester, New York. July, 1974

Moore, personal interview. Baltimore. March, 1974.

Stewart, Walker, personal interview. Genesee County. New York. 1959.

Thomas, Elder, personal interview. Bermuda. December 5, 1973.

Walker, Wyatt, personal interview. July 20. 1974. Rochester, New York.

Washington, C. J., personal observation. Richmond, Virginia. January 1, 1974.

Williams, Moses, personal interview. Baltimore, Maryland. March, 1974.

Baltimore Deacons' Union, personal interview. March 15, 1974.

Banks, Washington, personal interview. Baltimore, Maryland. November 15, 1973.

Gray, prayer heard by the writer. Norfolk, Virginia. August, 1961.

Higgins, I. Bradshaw, prayer heard by the writer. Baltimore, Maryland. February 17, 1972.

Johnson, Freeman, prayer heard by the writer. Lynchburg, Virginia, October, 1962.

Kilgore, Thomas, prayer heard by the writer. Chicago, Illinois. March, 1974

Ransome, W. L., prayer heard by the writer. Hampton, Virginia. June 8, 1973.

Youth, prayers heard by the writer. Baltimore, Maryland. 1974.

Traditional prayer lines.

Untitled Reports. M248 m96. Washington: Howard University Library. 1974.

Index